50 STRATEGIES for Cooperative Learning

Sabrina Winkleman, M.Ed.

To Ma—may the liberation you experienced on Walker's Creek continue to heal our lineage. Your love is a constant balm.

Publishing Credits

Corinne Burton, M.A.Ed., *President and Publisher*
Aubrie Nielsen, M.S.Ed., *EVP of Content Development*
Kyra Ostendorf, M.Ed., *Publisher, professional books*
Véronique Bos, *VP of Creative*
Alison Behnke, *Senior Editor*
Kevin Pham, *Graphic Designer*

Image Credits

All images from iStock and/or Shutterstock

Library of Congress Cataloging-in-Publication Data

Names: Winkleman, Sabrina, author.
Title: 50 strategies for cooperative learning / Sabrina Winkleman.
    Other titles: Fifty strategies for cooperative learning
Description: Huntington Beach, CA : Shell Educational Publishing, Inc.,
    2025. | Series: 50 strategies | Includes bibliographical references.
Identifiers: LCCN 2024039400 (print) | LCCN 2024039401 (ebook) | ISBN 9798765987612
    (paperback) | ISBN 9798765987629 (ebook) | ISBN 9798765987636 (epub)
Subjects: LCSH: Group work in education. | Affective education.
Classification: LCC LB1032 .W56 2025 (print) | LCC LB1032 (ebook) | DDC 371.3/6--
    dc23/eng/20240917
LC record available at https://lccn.loc.gov/2024039400
LC ebook record available at https://lccn.loc.gov/2024039401

A division of Teacher Created Materials
5482 Argosy Avenue
Huntington Beach, CA 92649-1039
www.tcmpub.com/shell-education
ISBN 979-8-7659-8761-2
© 2025 Shell Educational Publishing, Inc.

Printed by: **418**
Printed in: **USA** / PO#: **PO14004**

Table of Contents

Introduction

Strategies

Appendices

Welcome

What are your experiences with wholeness in education? How often do you consider and plan for the many domains of development: physical, psychological, cognitive, social, and emotional, particularly as they connect to your and your students' identities? How frequently do you think about the brain in relationship to the nervous system? And how might wholeness move us toward equitable learning environments where both adults and students thrive?

I know these aren't easy questions—yet I believe answering them is critical to your students' well-being and learning, as well as your own. And my hope is that the strategies in this book help you build and support the skills, habits, and mindsets needed to not just navigate but embrace wholeness. Wholeness honors the differences and complexities of humanity and moves us toward a more caring and just world.

Navigating wholeness has been a long journey for me. Slowly developing reflective practices like mindfulness and focusing on cultivating my own social and emotional skills are steps that have positively impacted my nervous system, mental health, and sense of joy and humility in the world. I find this particularly important as someone who has a high adverse childhood experiences (ACEs) score. The score is not destiny. I am proof, as are many others! High ACEs scores are not destiny for our students and communities either. When we choose to implement strategies that consider and welcome our students' wholeness, we create identity-affirming learning environments that protect against mental health risks, support joy, boost academics, and interrupt historical inequities.

Cooperative learning, alongside transformative social and emotional learning (tSEL), is a powerful way to practice wholeness in the classroom through its emphasis on student voice and collaboration. You probably already use many elements of both cooperative learning and social and emotional learning with your students. This book's simple and effective strategies emphasize the relationship between the two concepts, offering ways to create an identity-affirming learning environment that honors wholeness and well-being for all of us—adults included.

This book does not contain a list of basic cooperative learning lessons or activities. Instead, each strategy offers a way to explicitly pair a tSEL competency with the academic goals and objectives of any cooperative learning lesson. These strategies also highlight the importance of cooperative learning that is responsive to all student identities; the strategies are therefore centered in healing. This partnership of the tSEL strategy with your responsive cooperative learning lesson supports well-being for you and your students.

When I was a first grade teacher, this kind of partnership ensured both joyful engagement and academic growth. For example, my classroom co-constructed a call and response to use for SEL skill reflection at the end of a responsive cooperative learning lesson. Students looked forward to singing while referring to a visual list of SEL skills such as "work the whole time" and "try your best." I would sing the phrase, "Did you work the whole time?" Students would sing back "work the whole time" and give themselves a private, close-to-their-bodies thumbs-up, thumb to the side, or thumbs-down for reflection. These reflections often echoed success with academic goals and objectives associated with the responsive cooperative learning lesson.

Similarly, when I was a literacy specialist, community agreements paired with responsive cooperative learning lessons ensured both meaningful interaction and academic progress. Students led SEL reflection time at the end of cooperative learning lessons by volunteering to review our community agreements and provide examples of what went well and what could be improved for next time. Again, these reflections often echoed academic growth during a lesson. Truly, explicitly focusing on wholeness in this way cultivates a joyful classroom climate and leads to academic, social, and emotional success.

This wholeness approach prioritizes safety, belonging, and dignity for all—things I needed as a child and young person. Writing this book has been part of my journey toward my own healing. It is also a way for me to advocate for other educators to create learning environments that honor all of us as whole, unique individuals, so we can, in turn, restore our collective humanity. I wish you well on this powerful journey!

—Sabrina

Cooperative Learning, Transformative SEL, and Teaching with a Wholeness Lens

When we teach with a wholeness lens, we honor the dynamic relationships among physical, psychological, cognitive, social, and emotional development with regard to our students' identities. Responsive cooperative learning supports this wholeness through its conditions for connection. Adults and students learn to work together in co-constructed, significant ways that hold one another accountable for engaged, responsive learning. Everyone participating in a responsive cooperative learning lesson boosts their communication skills as they navigate ideas, opportunities, conflicts, roadblocks, resources, and perspectives. These conditions for connection offer opportunities to deepen relationships, center meaningful experiences, and amplify authentic learning, all of which, in turn, enhance a sense of belonging and agency in the classroom.

However, responsive cooperative learning's conditions for connection don't occur without intentional and explicit transformative SEL instruction. Social skills are the keys to connection, and transformative SEL is thus a key element in preparing and planning for responsive cooperative learning opportunities. As the Learning Policy Institute and Turnaround for Children, in partnership with the Forum for Youth Investment and in association with the Science of Learning and Development (SoLD) Alliance, noted in *Design Principles for Schools: Putting the Science of Learning and Development into Action*, "The primary energy source for the wiring of the brain is human connection; the neurochemicals and hormones that are released through human relationships are the fuel causing neurons to fire and connect" (2021, 87). Connection is the fuel for life and learning.

> As teachers, the greatest gift we can offer our students is our presence and our ability to see and accept them as they are.
>
> —Meena Srinivasan

Accessing this fuel is at the heart of every strategy in this book. When we intentionally use transformative social and emotional learning (tSEL) to support the conditions for the most effective, responsive cooperative learning, we prepare our students and ourselves to openly and thoughtfully engage in exploring academic content and making connections from regulated nervous systems. We are authentic, at ease, alert, and curious, and we anticipate joy in learning—conditions that support our mental health and well-being.

Before discussing this powerful partnership of responsive cooperative learning with transformative social and emotional learning, let's dig into some basics about each.

Defining Cooperative Learning

What is your personal experience with cooperative learning? How often do you remember engaging in it as a student? How regularly do you facilitate it in your classroom? Did you know that there are three main structures for cooperative learning groups? Are you familiar with the five essential elements associated with cooperative learning? Let's get into it!

David and Roger Johnson, codirectors of the Cooperative Learning Institute at the University of Minnesota, provide helpful parameters for cooperative learning (Johnson and Johnson, n.d.). Cooperative learning groups can be set up in three ways:

1. Informally, for short amounts of time for processing learning at any time during a lesson

2. Formally, for structured, longer-term complex tasks

3. As a base for long-term cooperation and support with personal or academic tasks, goals, and routines, such as class attendance and homework completion

> One of the goals of education is not simply to fill students with facts and information but to help them learn how to learn.
>
> —Zaretta Hammond

When using the strategies in this book, you'll likely pair them with the formal, structured style of group work. When planning these formal, responsive cooperative learning lessons, it's important to consider group size (three to five students per group is ideal), as well as specific, responsive academic goals and objectives that align with diverse student identities. These goals and objectives should incorporate five essential elements:

1. Positive interdependence (students working together toward a goal)

2. Accessing and applying social and emotional competencies

3. Individual accountability of each student

4. Promoting fellow group members' success in service of the lesson's goals

5. Group processing (time to reflect and debrief at the end of a lesson)

These five essential elements all rely heavily on social skills, which is why focusing on responsive cooperative learning through the lens of transformative social and emotional learning is so important and effective. Using this lens helps you create the conditions for a caring, just, and joyful learning environment where academic outcomes improve and relationships thrive through authentic communication and meaningful lesson content.

Defining Transformative SEL

What are your experiences with SEL? When and where did you learn about it? Have you ever thought of SEL as transformative? To better understand transformative SEL, let's consider SEL's five key competencies as defined by the Collaborative for Academic, Social, and Emotional Learning (CASEL) and the five associated concepts (which CASEL refers to as focal constructs) that make them transformative (CASEL, n.d.).

At its core, social and emotional learning is about our humanity—individually and collectively. How do we connect to ourselves and others? How do we process our experiences through our identities and emotions? How do we aspire to impact our communities and eradicate inequities? To help us answer these questions and build our students' and our own social and emotional skills, CASEL identifies the following five interrelated competencies we can cultivate on our journeys:

> Every child deserves an education that guarantees the safety to learn in the comfort of one's own skin.
>
> —Dena Simmons

- self-awareness
- self-management
- social awareness
- relationship skills
- responsible decision-making

These powerful competencies can be strengthened in students when we intentionally integrate them with instructional practices such as responsive cooperative learning. And they become transformative when we pair them with five related concepts of identity, agency, belonging, problem-solving, and curiosity. These five concepts provide the theme of each section of strategies in this book:

- self-awareness and identity
- self-management and agency
- social awareness and belonging
- relationship skills and problem-solving
- responsible decision-making and curiosity

Transformative SEL (tSEL) goes beyond SEL to center innovative strategies that strive to close long-standing gaps in educational opportunities and outcomes. It highlights our collective rights and our collective responsibilities for creating caring and just learning environments that honor our differences, particularly the differences of those who have been historically excluded from our educational systems.

Transformative SEL invites relationship-building based on co-learning between adults and students, and in turn, helps create caring and just learning environments that center student and community strengths, partnerships, and solutions for inequities. And it is, in large part, this focus on connection, affirmation, and collaboration that makes tSEL such a natural and effective partner to responsive cooperative learning.

Building the Relationship Between Cooperative Learning and Transformative SEL

As we explored in the previous sections, the foundational, essential elements of responsive cooperative learning all rely heavily on social skills that honor diverse student identities. By explicitly and intentionally approaching responsive cooperative learning through a tSEL mindset, we cultivate these social skills in service of creating a learning environment that is welcoming, affirming, and equitable—all while supporting academic skills and goals.

In this book, you will explore responsive cooperative learning through each of the five tSEL competencies and their associated concepts (or focal constructs). These competencies are dynamic and interconnected. However, separating them into individual competencies facilitates individual understanding first, followed by a deeper understanding of the relationships among them.

When you choose a strategy within a competency section, it becomes a tSEL anchor for your responsive cooperative learning lesson planning. Paired with the academic content you will cover, this anchor will support and build social skills needed for the lesson. This pairing supports a wholeness lens that considers diverse physical, psychological, cognitive, social, and emotional development in lesson planning, making even more effective use of your learning time and setting you and your students up for authenticity, engagement, and growth.

> " Cognitive, academic, social, and emotional development are inextricably linked.
>
> —Science of Learning and Development Alliance "

Intentional Strategy Design

As you navigate this book, you will find that every strategy relies on two core approaches: activation and reflection. Once you choose a strategy to focus on during a responsive cooperative learning lesson, you can choose an activation tool and a reflection tool to use as you teach the academic content of the lesson alongside tSEL. Taking this consistent approach to integrating responsive cooperative learning and tSEL eases students' cognitive load and allows you to focus on the key concept of each strategy in partnership with the academic content of your lesson. You can flip to any strategy and reduce your lesson prep time!

Each strategy is structured with a three-paragraph design (reducing *your* cognitive load!):

- First, an overview paragraph introduces the strategy's **focus** and **goals**.

- Next, a paragraph discusses how you can **activate** the strategy through brainstorming with students and looks at how this activation connects the strategy to your responsive cooperative learning lesson's academic goals and objectives. Activation recommendations are differentiated by grade level in the strategy's "Make It Real" section. On page 12, you'll find a list of Activation Tools to choose from—and of course you can also call upon other known favorites too.

- Finally, a third paragraph focuses on how your group can **reflect** at the end of your responsive cooperative learning lesson. On page 13, you'll find a list of Reflection Tools to choose from—but again, feel free to use other preferred reflection activities as well.

This intentional design ensures that you can implement these strategies in a predictable way given limited prep time. We can all deepen our learning through the power of routines—students and teachers alike.

Speaking of learning for teachers, be sure to also check out the Adult tSEL feature in each strategy. This feature invites you to model and grow your own transformative social and emotional skills alongside your students. Your wholeness is critically important for your life inside and outside the classroom, and your modeling of these skills will deeply impact your students.

Strategy Walkthrough

Let's walk through an example of how you can engage with this intentional design. Say you are planning a responsive cooperative learning lesson on exploring and analyzing the character traits of a protagonist in a story chosen to honor students' diverse identities. The main character is complex, and students have been having strong reactions to the character's choices in the story.

You decide that it's important for students to recognize and process their own emotions associated with the character, especially since their opinions about the character vary, so they need a strategy to navigate potential conflicts in their groups during the responsive cooperative learning lesson. You choose the "Honor Emotions" strategy on page 20 (in the Strengthening Self-Awareness to Cultivate Identity section) and pick an activation tool and a reflection tool from the lists on pages 12 and 13.

Next, you open the lesson by talking about your own emotions associated with the protagonist's traits. You encourage students to name their initial emotions through the activation tool and encourage them to continue naming their emotions as they explore and analyze the protagonist's traits with their small groups.

At the end of the lesson, the reflection tool helps students process how their feelings about the protagonist might have changed during the lesson and how their different, personal emotions may have played a role in their individual analysis of the main character's traits. You can share your own shifting emotional landscape during the lesson too!

Activation Tools

Activation tools support strategy brainstorming. I encourage you to be flexible with the tools and to scaffold according to your students' needs. For example, you may need to provide a sentence stem and visual for each strategy. You may need to model an example and then invite students to model as well. These scaffolds encourage whole-group engagement.

Anchor Charts: Anchor charts name the thoughts, ideas, and processes that you and your students will connect to a strategy. You and your students can co-construct an anchor chart as a whole group, or you might invite students to create anchor charts in their small groups. The chart (or charts) should remain visible during group learning for easy reference.

Journaling: Journaling provides an opportunity for individual processing of students' ideas connected to the strategy. Consider offering space for students to share their journaling thoughts with their small groups or as a whole group. This tool can also support private processing.

Sticky Notes: Sticky notes can be a way for students to anonymously connect their ideas to a strategy. Invite students to use their sticky notes to share their thoughts about a strategy and then anonymously place them in a location where you can process them.

Turn and Talk: Turn and Talk encourages verbal processing of ideas connected to the strategy. Students physically turn and chat with a student or students near them to brainstorm their collective thoughts about the strategy. Consider also offering time for pairs to voluntarily share with the whole group.

Think-Pair-Share: Think-Pair-Share honors individual think time along with collaborative verbal processing and sharing of the strategy. Provide individual, silent time for students to brainstorm their thoughts associated with the strategy, then provide time for them to pair up and verbally share their ideas. Consider offering time for pairs to voluntarily share with the whole group.

Hands-Up, Pair Up: Hands-Up, Pair Up encourages movement, inclusion, and verbal processing. Invite students to raise their hands and move around the classroom to pair up. You will know when everyone is paired up when you see all hands paired in the air. Once that occurs, invite students to chat about their ideas connected to the strategy. Consider offering time for pairs to voluntarily share with the whole group.

Pencil Talk: Pencil Talk provides a silent space for students to share their thoughts about a strategy. Consider posting multiple charts around the room or titling multiple sections of the board with the strategy. Invite students to let their pencils "talk" about the strategy by noting their ideas on the posters or with sticky notes for the board. Consider inviting a student to read the group's collective thoughts aloud.

Reflection Tools

Reflection tools support learning synthesis, engagement, and growth. They provide a space for students to actively reflect on what went well during the cooperative learning lesson and what could go better next time. Reflection tools support student voice and meaning making.

Whole-Class Discussion: Whole-class discussions invite students to engage in the strategy reflection questions collectively. Post the questions in a spot visible to all and consider providing a couple of minutes for individual, silent reflection before opening it up for a whole-class discussion.

Small-Group Discussion: Small-group discussions invite students to engage with the strategy reflection questions in their small groups. Encourage all group members to participate and consider offering a couple of minutes of individual, silent reflection before beginning the discussion. Circulate among the groups and take note of students' reflections.

Journaling: Journaling provides a private way to process the strategy reflection questions and can offer a physical space for you to consider and review students' individual processing. Consider your capacity to provide feedback on students' strategy reflection questions.

Creating Art: Creating art associated with the strategy reflection questions offers a creative venue for self-expression. Provide materials (such as markers, paper, clay, pipe cleaners, and so on) and consider inviting students to share their art with one another.

Exit Slips: Exit slips provide a written artifact of students' strategy reflections. Consider printing the reflection questions on cards. Students can then hand their answers in at the end of each cooperative learning lesson.

What Next?: What Next? provides the opportunity for students to process the strategy reflection questions and then consider how they will apply their reflections to other areas of their life. Post the strategy reflection questions, offer time for processing, and then ask students how they will use their reflections in other areas of their lives.

Still Wondering: Still Wondering provides space for students to process the strategy reflection questions and then note what they are still wondering about the strategy, which encourages a classroom climate of curiosity. Post the strategy reflection questions, offer time for processing, and then ask students what elements of the strategy they are still wondering about.

Digital Content

At the end of the book, you'll learn how to access a list of digital articles associated with the strategies in the book. These articles are practical, research-based quick-reads to further your interest in a particular strategy. Many contain tangible examples. I hope they will be helpful, efficient references for you!

Cultivating Your Own Transformative SEL Skills for Facilitating Cooperative Learning

As educators, our mental health and well-being are central to our own wholeness and therefore to our ability to navigate wholeness in our classrooms. We are powerful models of tSEL for our students and can build on this truth to create the learning conditions for all to thrive. Each strategy in this book incorporates adult reflections centered on the strategy's tSEL skill, which will strengthen your own tSEL skills alongside those of your students.

When facilitating responsive cooperative learning lessons, cultivating your own tSEL has multiple benefits. You engage in healthy communication with and alongside your students. Just as their empathy, patience, and kindness increase, so do yours. Your cultural competence and responsiveness deepen, as well, by considering how your own identities shape your facilitation and creation of lessons.

Engaging with responsive cooperative learning through the lens of tSEL supports and affirms the wholeness of your students, explicitly and intentionally pairing social skills with academic learning. This wholeness is for you too. By strengthening your skills within tSEL's concepts of identity, agency, belonging, collaborative problem-solving, and curiosity, you deepen your humanity along with that of the students you teach.

> "
> *Through practicing self-reflection and self-awareness, developing cultural humility, and gaining exposure to culturally responsive pedagogy, educators can expand their knowledge of how to use SEL to humanize and honor all students.*
>
> —Meiko Lin, Svea Olsen, Dena N. Simmons, Miriam Miller, and Shauna L. Tominey
> "

How to Use This Resource

Choose a strategy and give it a try! And of course, you know your group best—so don't hesitate to modify these strategies to suit your students' unique needs. All the strategies in this book are designed to be flexible and to apply to all grade levels and topics.

This introductory text provides a description of the strategy.

Differentiation ideas are provided for three grade ranges.

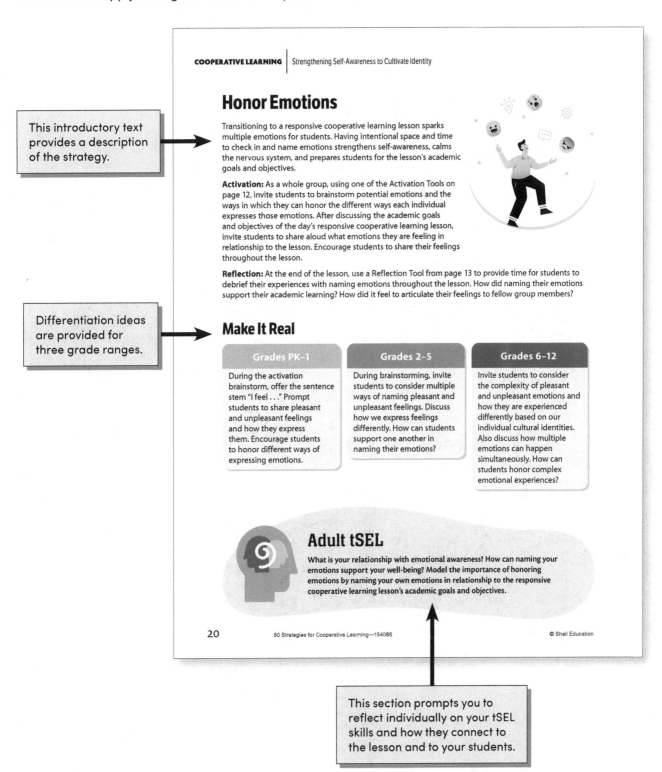

COOPERATIVE LEARNING | Strengthening Self-Awareness to Cultivate Identity

Honor Emotions

Transitioning to a responsive cooperative learning lesson sparks multiple emotions for students. Having intentional space and time to check in and name emotions strengthens self-awareness, calms the nervous system, and prepares students for the lesson's academic goals and objectives.

Activation: As a whole group, using one of the Activation Tools on page 12, invite students to brainstorm potential emotions and the ways in which they can honor the different ways each individual expresses those emotions. After discussing the academic goals and objectives of the day's responsive cooperative learning lesson, invite students to share aloud what emotions they are feeling in relationship to the lesson. Encourage students to share their feelings throughout the lesson.

Reflection: At the end of the lesson, use a Reflection Tool from page 13 to provide time for students to debrief their experiences with naming emotions throughout the lesson. How did naming their emotions support their academic learning? How did it feel to articulate their feelings to fellow group members?

Make It Real

Grades PK–1	Grades 2–5	Grades 6–12
During the activation brainstorm, offer the sentence stem "I feel . . ." Prompt students to share pleasant and unpleasant feelings and how they express them. Encourage students to honor different ways of expressing emotions.	During brainstorming, invite students to consider multiple ways of naming pleasant and unpleasant feelings. Discuss how we express feelings differently. How can students support one another in naming their emotions?	Invite students to consider the complexity of pleasant and unpleasant emotions and how they are experienced differently based on our individual cultural identities. Also discuss how multiple emotions can happen simultaneously. How can students honor complex emotional experiences?

Adult tSEL

What is your relationship with emotional awareness? How can naming your emotions support your well-being? Model the importance of honoring emotions by naming your own emotions in relationship to the responsive cooperative learning lesson's academic goals and objectives.

20   50 Strategies for Cooperative Learning—154085   © Shell Education

This section prompts you to reflect individually on your tSEL skills and how they connect to the lesson and to your students.

Strategies Table of Contents

Strengthening Self-Awareness to Cultivate Identity

When we center the concept of identity alongside self-awareness, we explore how we perceive ourselves as individuals and also as part of the communities around us. Having a clear sense of self supports our ability to navigate adversity, to interrupt inequities, and to develop holistically (academically, socially, and emotionally). When you choose a strategy from this section and pair its tSEL lens with academic goals and objectives, you encourage this identity development in your students (and yourself) during responsive cooperative learning lessons and beyond.

The Strategies

NAME:

Honor Emotions

Transitioning to a responsive cooperative learning lesson sparks multiple emotions for students. Having intentional space and time to check in and name emotions strengthens self-awareness, calms the nervous system, and prepares students for the lesson's academic goals and objectives.

Activation: As a whole group, using one of the Activation Tools on page 12, invite students to brainstorm potential emotions and the ways in which they can honor the different ways each individual expresses those emotions. After discussing the academic goals and objectives of the day's responsive cooperative learning lesson, invite students to share aloud what emotions they are feeling in relationship to the lesson. Encourage students to share their feelings throughout the lesson.

Reflection: At the end of the lesson, use a Reflection Tool from page 13 to provide time for students to debrief their experiences with naming emotions throughout the lesson. How did naming their emotions support their academic learning? How did it feel to articulate their feelings to fellow group members?

Make It Real

Grades PK–1	Grades 2–5	Grades 6–12
During the activation brainstorm, offer the sentence stem "I feel . . ." Prompt students to share pleasant and unpleasant feelings and how they express them. Encourage students to honor different ways of expressing emotions.	During brainstorming, invite students to consider multiple ways of naming pleasant and unpleasant feelings. Discuss how we express feelings differently. How can students support one another in naming their emotions?	Invite students to consider the complexity of pleasant and unpleasant emotions and how they are experienced differently based on our individual cultural identities. Also discuss how multiple emotions can happen simultaneously. How can students honor complex emotional experiences?

Adult tSEL

What is your relationship with emotional awareness? How can naming your emotions support your well-being? Model the importance of honoring emotions by naming your own emotions in relationship to the responsive cooperative learning lesson's academic goals and objectives.

Superpower Selection

All of us have strengths. Inviting students to name and use their personal strengths during responsive cooperative learning lessons increases self-esteem, fosters well-being, and builds confidence in meeting academic goals and objectives. These benefits in turn strengthen self-awareness.

Activation: Using one of the Activation Tools on page 12, invite students to brainstorm their strengths as superpowers. After discussing the academic goals and objectives of the day's responsive cooperative learning lesson, invite students to share aloud what superpowers they will use during the lesson.

Reflection: At the end of the lesson, use a Reflection Tool from page 13 to provide time for students to debrief their experiences using their superpowers throughout the lesson. How did their superpowers support their academic learning? How did their superpowers shift throughout the activity?

Make It Real

Grades PK–1	Grades 2–5	Grades 6–12
During the activation brainstorm, offer the sentence stem "My superpower is . . ." For example, "My superpower is being kind" or "My superpower is being creative."	Invite students to consider their superpowers in relationship to times when they've felt like the best versions of themselves. How did their superpowers impact their communities and themselves?	Ask students to consider the superpowers of the changemakers they most admire. How do students' own strengths mirror those of the people who've made a difference in their communities and in the world?

Adult tSEL

What is your relationship with identifying personal strengths? How can naming your personal superpowers support your well-being? Model a strength-based mindset by telling students what superpowers will support you during the responsive cooperative learning lesson.

Journal Reflections

Having a consistent place to capture personal needs during responsive cooperative learning cultivates safety. A journal can serve as an artifact to remind students of the importance of asking for and anticipating where they may need assistance during responsive cooperative learning lessons.

Activation: As a whole group, using one of the Activation Tools on page 12, invite students to brainstorm potential needs during responsive cooperative learning lessons. This might feel vulnerable to students, so encourage them to remember that it's important to articulate needs in order to receive community support. After discussing the academic goals and objectives of the day's responsive cooperative learning lesson, invite students to share aloud potential needs they would like to note in their journals.

Reflection: At the end of the lesson, use one of the Reflection Tools on page 13 to provide time for students to share their experiences. How did naming their needs support their academic learning? How was anticipating their needs in their journals helpful? How might they reflect on the experience in their journals?

Make It Real

Grades PK–1	Grades 2–5	Grades 6–12
During the activation brainstorm, offer the sentence stems "Someone might need . . ." and "I might need . . ." For example, "Someone might need a pencil." "I might need to keep trying." Students may draw, write, or dictate their chosen needs in their journals.	Invite students to consider emotional and physical needs. How can their journals be a place for them to note their needs for emotional support? What are the physical materials and/or supports they might need?	Encourage students to consider the role of vulnerability in expressing needs. How can their journals be a place for them to be honest about their needs and trust that their group members will support them?

Adult tSEL

What is your relationship with expressing your needs? How can expressing your needs support your well-being? Model the importance of naming your needs by sharing aloud your anticipated needs for the day's responsive cooperative learning lesson.

Making Mistakes

Creating a classroom community that embraces mistakes supports confidence and growth. Responsive cooperative learning offers an opportunity to encourage students to plan for and navigate mistakes, including being aware of and prepared for the feelings that may arise alongside them.

Activation: Using one of the Activation Tools on page 12, invite students to brainstorm what they can do when they make mistakes. After discussing the academic goals and objectives of the day's responsive cooperative learning lesson, invite students to share aloud what mistakes they might make during the lesson.

Reflection: At the end of the lesson, use one of the Reflection Tools on page 13 to provide time for students to discuss their experiences with mistakes. How did mistakes impact their academic learning? How did anticipating what to do when they make a mistake support their group work?

Make It Real

Grades PK–1	Grades 2–5	Grades 6–12
During the activation brainstorm, offer the sentence stem "When I make a mistake, I can . . ." For example, "When I make a mistake, I can try again" and "When I make a mistake, I can ask for help."	Invite students to brainstorm how to respond to emotions that might arise after making mistakes. What can students do if they feel upset when they make a mistake? How can they encourage themselves?	Invite students to brainstorm how to navigate any discomfort they have around making mistakes. How can students move through their discomfort in order to grow? How can they encourage one another?

Adult tSEL

What is your relationship with making mistakes? How can making mistakes support your growth? Model the importance of making mistakes by naming potential mistakes that could happen during the responsive cooperative learning lesson and how you might respond to them.

Focused Breathing for Mindful Transitions

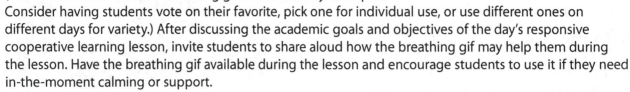

Transitioning between spaces and tasks may feel overwhelming, exciting, or unsettling to students. Intentional time to settle into learning calms the nervous system, encourages self-awareness, and prepares students for learning. Focused breathing provides an ever-available strategy to support this process and to help students tune into their bodies and minds.

Activation: Using one of the Activation Tools on page 12, invite students to brainstorm about focused breathing during transitions. (Search online for "mindful breathing gifs" to find many examples. Consider having students vote on their favorite, pick one for individual use, or use different ones on different days for variety.) After discussing the academic goals and objectives of the day's responsive cooperative learning lesson, invite students to share aloud how the breathing gif may help them during the lesson. Have the breathing gif available during the lesson and encourage students to use it if they need in-the-moment calming or support.

Reflection: At the end of the lesson, use one of the Reflection Tools on page 13 to provide time for students to discuss and reflect on their experiences using focused breathing during the lesson. How did it feel? How did it support them in the day's learning? What are other times and places they might use this breathing strategy?

Make It Real

Grades PK–1	Grades 2–5	Grades 6–12
During the activation brainstorm, offer the sentence stem "The breathing gif helps me . . ." For example, "The breathing gif helps me calm down," "relax," or "refocus."	Invite students to consider the simplicity of breathing with the gif and think about how it will be helpful. List their ideas. How can focusing on their breathing reset and refocus their experiences?	Invite students to consider the power of breathing in sync with the gif. List their thoughts. How does focused breathing help them experience the world differently?

Adult tSEL

What is your relationship with focused breathing? How can focused breathing support your well-being? Model focused breathing with your students and practice with their preferred gifs. Tell students how you feel after five breaths and ask them how their bodies feel.

Star Role

Responsive cooperative learning lessons offer space to explore and use group roles that strengthen self-awareness. These roles provide structure and purpose, as well as opportunities for growth. Invite students to identify and choose roles that align with their strengths and those that feel more challenging to them. Encourage students to be flexible with choosing roles and to take risks within the safety of their groups.

Activation: Using one of the Activation Tools on page 12, invite students to brainstorm star roles associated with responsive cooperative learning lessons, such as inquirer, materials manager, facilitator, speaker, encourager, timekeeper, recorder, and so on. After discussing the academic goals and objectives of the day's responsive cooperative learning lesson, invite students to share aloud what roles they might choose during the lesson.

Reflection: At the end of the lesson, use one of the Reflection Tools on page 13 to provide time for students to reflect on their experiences with their roles. How did choosing roles support their groups' collaborations, as well as students' individual academic learning? How did their strengths help them in their roles—whether the roles were comfortable or challenging for them?

Make It Real

Grades PK–1	Grades 2–5	Grades 6–12
During the activation brainstorm, offer the sentence stem "A group role is . . ." For example, "A group role is materials manager" or "A group role is recorder."	Invite students to consider how naming and choosing roles strengthens their connection to learning. First, list their role ideas. Then, discuss how roles give meaning to their learning.	Invite students to consider how roles support community and purpose. First, list their role ideas. Then, discuss how group roles ensure inclusivity.

Adult tSEL

What is your relationship with choosing roles that align with your strengths and those that challenge you? How can building on strengths and also taking healthy risks support your well-being? Model the importance of roles by sharing with students what role you will choose for yourself during the lesson.

Interest Inventory

Knowing your students' interests deepens your relationship with them and provides an opportunity to create engaging and responsive content for responsive cooperative learning lessons. Invite students to share their interests with you—and with each other—through interest inventories, strengthening their collective self-awareness. These inventories can be as specific or open-ended as you like. You may also choose to do this more than once a year to see if and how students' interests evolve.

Activation: As a whole group, using one of the Activation Tools on page 12, invite students to brainstorm an interest inventory listing some of their collective interests. After discussing the academic goals and objectives of the day's responsive cooperative learning lesson, invite students to share aloud which interests connect to the lesson.

Reflection: At the end of the lesson, use one of the Reflection Tools on page 13 to provide time for students to share their experiences with connecting their collective interests to their learning. What impact did this have on their academic learning? Their enjoyment of the lesson? Their connection with their group members?

Make It Real

Grades PK–1	Grades 2–5	Grades 6–12
During the activation brainstorm, offer the sentence stem "I like to . . ." For example, "I like to explore nature," "I like to play games," or "I like to make new friends."	Brainstorm and list student interests. How are students' different interests connected to each other? Which interests specifically connect to the responsive cooperative learning lesson?	Brainstorm and list student interests. How are students' interests connected to the classroom? What patterns are present in their collective interests? Do students have new interests based on their peers' responses?

Adult tSEL

What is your relationship with reflecting on and naming your interests? How can centering your interests support your well-being? Model the importance of reflecting on and naming your interests by sharing what excites you about the day's responsive cooperative learning lesson. If you'd like, you can also talk about ways your interests overlap with those of your students.

Values View

Aligning personal values with responsive cooperative learning lessons supports confidence, strengthens self-awareness, and makes lessons more meaningful. Inviting students to name their values increases connection and engagement in the classroom, particularly during responsive cooperative learning opportunities.

Activation: As a whole group, using one of the Activation Tools on page 12, invite students to brainstorm their collective values. After discussing the academic goals and objectives of the day's responsive cooperative learning lesson, invite students to share aloud what values they will use in relationship to the lesson.

Reflection: At the end of the lesson, use one of the Reflection Tools on page 13 to provide time for students to debrief their experiences. How did their personal values support their academic learning today? How did their values help them in their collaborative work with their groups?

Make It Real

Grades PK–1	Grades 2–5	Grades 6–12
To help students consider and identify values during the activation brainstorm, offer the sentence stem "I am proud to be . . ." For example, "I am proud to be caring."	Have students gather in their small groups to brainstorm their lists of values. If they need help getting started, invite them to focus on aspects of themselves they feel proud of and to use these ideas to identify values. For example, if a student is proud of their artwork, they might value creativity.	Encourage students to specifically consider how their values can help them during learning. For example, if they value enthusiasm, they might help their group stay positive during their work together. If they value communication, they might help make sure everyone is understanding each other as they collaborate.

Adult tSEL

What is your relationship with your personal values? How can aligning your personal values with teaching impact your well-being? Model the importance of aligning values to learning by sharing one or more values you will use during the responsive cooperative learning lesson.

Cultural Connection

Every student—and every educator—brings their cultural identities to the classroom. To create an identity-affirming learning environment, it's essential to honor the individual, family, and community symbols, languages, ways of being (norms), and customs that make up our collective humanity and celebrate our human rights.

Activation: Using one of the Activation Tools on page 12, invite students to brainstorm some of the elements of their cultures that are important and meaningful to them. After discussing the academic goals and objectives of the day's responsive cooperative learning lesson, invite students to share aloud what aspects of their cultural identities will support them during the lesson.

Reflection: At the end of the lesson, use one of the Reflection Tools on page 13 to provide time for students to share their experiences. How did it feel to consider and celebrate aspects of their cultures during the lesson? How did their cultural identities support their academic learning?

Make It Real

Grades PK–1	Grades 2–5	Grades 6–12
During the brainstorm activation, offer the sentence stem, "My family likes to . . ." For example, "My family likes to laugh," "My family likes to play," or "My family likes to share meals."	Invite students to work individually first to list their cultural aspects, then share with their small groups, and finally share with the whole group. Some ideas may include "We joke a lot," "We work hard," and "We celebrate together."	Invite students to work individually first to list their cultural aspects, then share with their small groups, and finally share with the whole group. Discuss how cultures connect and how they are different. How can students honor each other's cultures?

Adult tSEL

What is your relationship with your own cultural identities? How can reflecting on, naming, and celebrating aspects of your cultural identities support your well-being? Model your personal cultural awareness by sharing something from your cultural identities that you will use during the responsive cooperative learning lesson.

Confidence Comfort

Approaching new learning with confidence supports students' optimism, perseverance, and flexibility, which in turn supports their self-awareness. Responsive cooperative learning lessons offer a space for students to build confidence through anticipating challenges and developing a plan for navigating them.

Activation: As a whole group, using one of the Activation Tools on page 12, invite students to brainstorm ways they are confident. After discussing the academic goals and objectives of the day's responsive cooperative learning lesson, invite students to share aloud the ways they can be confident during the lesson.

Reflection: At the end of the lesson, use one of the Reflection Tools on page 13 to provide time for students to debrief their experiences with confidence. How did their confidence support their academic learning? What strategies did they use to persevere? How are they growing in their ability to trust themselves?

Make It Real

Grades PK–1	Grades 2–5	Grades 6–12
During the brainstorm activation, offer the sentence stem "I am confident because . . ." For example, "I am confident because I trust myself" or "I am confident because if I fail, I will try again."	As they brainstorm ideas, encourage students to include details about why they feel confident in the areas they do—whether it's their ability to be curious, persevere, respond to mistakes, or other reasons.	Invite students to offer ideas that center trusting themselves to navigate challenges by naming specific strategies and strengths that will help them overcome potential barriers.

Adult tSEL

What is your relationship with confidence? How can approaching new learning with confidence support your well-being? Model your confidence before a responsive cooperative learning lesson by explicitly naming the challenges ahead, how you will persevere, and how you will navigate mistakes.

Strengthening Self-Management to Cultivate Agency

When we help our students develop agency—the sense that they have some control over their lives, along with the ability to handle what comes their way—we also help them gain and strengthen self-management skills. These skills are crucial for responsive cooperative learning, and they also help us discover new ways to make a difference in our classrooms, our responsive cooperative learning groups, and our communities. Self-management helps us reflect and take action toward our goals and in areas of personal growth. When you choose a strategy from this section and pair its tSEL lens with academic goals and objectives, you support this development of personal agency in your students (and yourself) during responsive cooperative learning lessons and beyond.

The Strategies

Intention-Setting

Intention-setting is a great opportunity to encourage mindfulness and agency during responsive cooperative learning lessons. Having the time and space to name our intentions for our actions and behaviors primes our neural system to respond in those ways and provides a sense of personal direction and self-management during learning.

Activation: Using one of the Activation Tools on page 12, invite students to brainstorm their potential intentions for learning. After discussing the academic goals and objectives of the day's responsive cooperative learning lesson, invite students to share aloud which intention will support them during the lesson.

Reflection: At the end of the lesson, use one of the Reflection Tools on page 13 to provide time for students to share about their experiences with intention-setting. How did naming their intentions support their academic learning? Was following through on their intentions challenging in any way?

Make It Real

Grades PK–1	Grades 2–5	Grades 6–12
During the activation brainstorm, offer the sentence stem "I want to . . ." For example, "I want to listen to my group," "I want to focus," or "I want to have fun."	Invite students to consider what version of themselves they would like to be in order to maximize their learning. List their ideas. Discuss what is the best version of themselves that they would like to bring to their small groups.	Invite students to consider their aspirations for themselves, in general. List their ideas. Discuss how intention-setting impacts all aspects of our lives. What intentions support the people students would like to be in the world?

Adult tSEL

What is your relationship with intention-setting? How can the practice support your well-being? Model the importance of naming intentions by sharing one of your intentions for the day's responsive cooperative learning lesson.

Stress Strategies

Stress is a part of life, and having strategies to respond instead of react to daily stressors boosts our sense of influence and agency over our lives, which deepens our self-management skills. To support students' stress management, encourage them to pause when they are stressed, name their feelings, and choose a helpful action.

Activation: Using one of the Activation Tools on page 12, invite students to brainstorm what they can do when they feel stress. After discussing the academic goals and objectives of the day's responsive cooperative learning lesson, invite students to share aloud what they can do when they feel stress during the lesson.

Reflection: At the end of the lesson, use one of the Reflection Tools on page 13 to provide time for students to discuss their experiences. How did their stress strategies support their academic learning? How did students navigate obstacles or conflicts during their group work?

Make It Real

Grades PK–1	Grades 2–5	Grades 6–12
During the activation brainstorm, offer the sentence stem "When I feel stressed, I . . ." For example, "When I feel stressed, I take deep breaths," or "When I feel stressed, I wiggle my body."	Invite students to work in their small groups. Prompt students to discuss how they can support each other with stress. What stress strategies do they think will be most effective for them? How could moving their bodies be helpful?	Invite students to work in their small groups. Prompt students to discuss examples of when stress can be helpful and when it is more harmful. What strategies can they use to support each other when they feel dysregulated?

Adult tSEL

What is your relationship with stress? How can explicitly navigating stress support your well-being? Model navigating stress by sharing the "Pause, Name, Choose" stress plan you'll use for the day's responsive cooperative learning lesson.

Step Success

Having clear academic goals and objectives for a responsive cooperative learning lesson provides a planned path toward achievement. Creating a step-by-step process for accomplishing learning goals and objectives supports students' sense of agency and readies them for success. This strengthens their self-management skills.

Activation: Using one of the Activation Tools on page 12, invite students to brainstorm general steps for completing responsive cooperative learning lessons generally. After discussing the academic goals and objectives of the day's responsive cooperative learning lesson, invite students to share aloud the necessary steps for completing the lesson.

Reflection: At the end of the lesson, use one of the Reflection Tools on page 13 to provide time for students to talk about their experiences with step success. How did their step-by-step plans support their academic learning? Did they feel a greater sense of confidence and agency when they approached the work with these plans? How might things have gone differently if they hadn't had the planned steps?

Make It Real

Grades PK–1	Grades 2–5	Grades 6–12
During the activation brainstorm, suggest students focus on a three-step process. For example, "First, we look at the goal. Then, we get supplies. Finally, we work together to finish." Invite students to share what step they are most excited about and why.	Suggest students think about five to seven steps to complete academic learning goals. Invite students to consider what steps they are excited about or feel unsure about, and why.	Invite students to consider three main steps each for the beginning, middle, and end of a lesson in relationship to its posted learning goals. How can students use backward planning (starting from the learning goals) to support their success?

Adult tSEL

What is your relationship with goal-setting and planning for success in reaching those goals? How can explicitly naming goals, as well as project steps in service of your goals, support your well-being? Model the importance of explicitly naming project steps by sharing your personal steps for the responsive cooperative learning lesson.

Inspecting Time

Explicitly reflecting on time supports cooperative learning goals and builds the self-management skills of anticipating, budgeting, and tracking time. When students plan for the time involved in responsive cooperative learning lessons and follow through by monitoring their time, they develop the ability to adjust their actions, whether time is running short or they're ahead of their expected schedule.

Activation: Using one of the Activation Tools on page 12, invite students to brainstorm ways a timer could be helpful during group work. Display a physical or online timer and show how it will work during learning. After discussing the academic goals and objectives of the day's responsive cooperative learning lesson, invite students to share aloud how they will use the timer during the lesson.

Reflection: At the end of the lesson, use one of the Reflection Tools on page 13 to provide time for students to debrief their experiences with the timer. How did the timer support their academic learning? Did they find using it difficult in any way? Are there ways they'd use it differently in future cooperative learning lessons?

Make It Real

Grades PK–1	Grades 2–5	Grades 6–12
During the activation brainstorm, offer the sentence stem "Timers are important because . . ." For example, "Timers are important because they help us know how much time is left" or "Timers are important because they help us pace ourselves."	Invite students to consider how the timer can support their group's efforts, how they can be flexible with it, and how they can use it to monitor themselves.	Invite students to consider how the use of the timer might yield surprises and how they can use their experiences to inform future lessons.

Adult tSEL

What is your relationship with time management? How can the practice support your well-being? Model the importance of time management by sharing your time management plan for the day's responsive cooperative learning lesson.

Contract Creation

Creating a contract for success for a responsive cooperative learning lesson supports engagement, inspiration, and confidence. It may support and/or align with other contracts you create with your students in different contexts, such as at the beginning of the year, with individuals, with grade levels, and so on. Adhering to this contract for success also helps students cultivate self-management skills. Invite students to reflect on what actions, steps, or mindsets they believe will support their success during responsive cooperative learning lessons.

Activation: As a whole group, using one of the Activation Tools on page 12, invite students to brainstorm what commitments they believe will set them up for learning success. After discussing the academic goals and objectives of the day's responsive cooperative learning lesson, invite students to share aloud what commitments they want to focus on during the lesson.

Reflection: At the end of the lesson, use one of the Reflection Tools on page 13 to provide time for students to discuss their experiences using their contract for success. How did commitments they made bolster their learning, both individually and as members of their groups? How did they do with fulfilling their commitments—and if they didn't meet their promises, what can they do differently next time?

Make It Real

Grades PK–1	Grades 2–5	Grades 6–12
During the activation brainstorm, offer the sentence stem "I promise to . . ." For example, "I promise to try my best," "I promise to get started right away," or "I promise to help others."	Invite students to consider ideas with depth. In students' heart of hearts, what commitments do they believe would best support their learning in their groups?	Invite students to consider their roles as members of their small-group ecosystems. How do students' commitments support the ecosystem of their groups?

Adult tSEL

What is your relationship with learning contracts? Have you used them to direct and inspire your own learning? How might the practice support your well-being? Model the importance of a learning contract by sharing your personal promises or agreements for the responsive cooperative learning lesson.

Checklists

Personal checklists help inspire and motivate students to achieve a responsive cooperative learning lesson's academic goals and objectives and organize their approaches to tasks. With students, discuss how checklists provide a sense of accomplishment and focus, which in turn, impacts well-being and strengthens self-management skills.

Activation: Using one of the Activation Tools on page 12, invite students to brainstorm important items associated with responsive cooperative learning lessons. After discussing the academic goals and objectives of the day's responsive cooperative learning lesson, invite students to share aloud the important items needed for the lesson.

Reflection: At the end of the lesson, use one of the Reflection Tools on page 13 to provide time for students to debrief their experiences with the checklist. How did the items on the list help them meet their academic goals? How did the items support their perseverance and sense of direction?

Make It Real

Grades PK–1	Grades 2–5	Grades 6–12
During the activation brainstorm, offer a "first, next, finally" structure. For example, "First we look at the learning goal and give a thumbs-up if we understand. Next, we follow the directions as a group and make a checkmark in the air when we're done. Finally, we look at the learning goal again and give a thumbs-up if we met the goal."	Invite students to consider the commonalities of all responsive cooperative learning lessons. Have them discuss the key items involved. What routines are always followed, and what do students need to remember?	Invite students to consider important items associated with the beginning, middle, and end of all responsive cooperative learning lessons. How can students create a broad checklist that encompasses the commonalities?

Adult tSEL

What is your relationship with checklists? How can using checklists support your well-being? Model the importance of a checklist by sharing your personal checklist for the day's responsive cooperative learning lesson.

Create Courage

Responsive cooperative learning lessons involve vulnerability, stepping into the potential for growth, and risk-taking. Encouraging students to name strategies for supporting their courage develops their sense of agency and confidence, deepening their self-management skills.

Activation: Using one of the Activation Tools on page 12, invite students to brainstorm ways they can be courageous during responsive cooperative learning lessons. After discussing the academic goals and objectives of the day's responsive cooperative learning lesson, invite students to share aloud how they can be courageous during the lesson.

Reflection: At the end of the lesson, use one of the Reflection Tools on page 13 to provide time for students to share their experiences with building courage. How did courage support them during today's lesson? How did it feel to be courageous? How will they be courageous next time?

Make It Real

Grades PK–1	Grades 2–5	Grades 6–12
During the activation brainstorm, offer the sentence stem "I am courageous when I . . ." For example, "I am courageous when I try new things," or "I am courageous when I try to speak up more." Consider using a visual such as a lion to scaffold students' understanding of the meaning of courage.	Invite students to brainstorm moments when they've been courageous and the risks they took. How did they decide to have courage to try something new? How can they support one another when they are trying to be courageous?	Invite students to brainstorm about the importance of courage. How are courage and learning related? What would happen if we didn't decide to be courageous?

Adult tSEL

What is your relationship with courage? How can courage support your well-being? Model the importance of courage by sharing at least one way you plan to be courageous during the responsive cooperative learning lesson.

Organize It

Responsive cooperative learning lessons offer a wealth of opportunities for students to strengthen their organizational skills. Supporting their efforts to organize their bodies and materials—individually and in their small groups—contributes to a sense of safety in the classroom and builds confidence.

Activation: Using one of the Activation Tools on page 12, invite students to brainstorm important body and material items associated with responsive cooperative learning lessons. After discussing the academic goals and objectives of the day's responsive cooperative learning lesson, invite students to share aloud what organizational items they need for the lesson.

Reflection: At the end of the lesson, use one of the Reflection Tools on page 13 to provide time for students to discuss their experiences with their organizational items. How did the items support their academic learning? Did they need to be flexible with anything? What might they change for next time?

Make It Real

Grades PK–1	Grades 2–5	Grades 6–12
During the activation brainstorm, offer two areas, one with the title "What Our Bodies Need" (for example, "space to stretch" or "space to work") and one titled "What Materials We Need" (for example, "pencils" or "manipulatives").	Invite students to consider the spatial needs of their bodies and the physical materials that support their learning. How do physical materials set students up for success? How do students share physical space with their group members?	Invite students to consider how to organize themselves physically and emotionally. How do students organize their mindsets for responsive cooperative learning lessons? What's the importance of considering physical space and other materials?

Adult tSEL

What is your relationship with organizational skills? How can being organized support your well-being? Model the importance of organizational skills by sharing your anticipated needs for your body and for physical materials during the responsive cooperative learning lesson.

Flex

Monitoring and adjusting our approaches and mindsets are important elements of cooperative learning lessons. Inviting students to pursue flexible thinking strengthens their self-management skills while boosting their sense of agency, supporting curiosity, and creating connections.

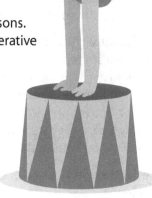

Activation: Using one of the Activation Tools on page 12, invite students to brainstorm ways they can be flexible during responsive cooperative learning lessons. After discussing the academic goals and objectives of the day's responsive cooperative learning lesson, invite students to share aloud ways of being flexible during the lesson.

Reflection: At the end of the lesson, use one of the Reflection Tools on page 13 to provide time for students to debrief their experiences with flexibility. How did their flexibility support their academic learning? How did it feel to work on being flexible? How could flexible thinking help them in other areas of their lives?

Make It Real

Grades PK–1	Grades 2–5	Grades 6–12
During the activation brainstorm, encourage students to think of ways they can go with the flow and be flexible during the lesson. For example, "I can wait for my turn," "I will take deep breaths if I'm frustrated," or "I know that I will make mistakes, and that's okay."	Invite students to consider the importance of being flexible. What if group members want to try something different? What if group members run out of materials? What happens if students run out of time?	Invite students to consider the role of monitoring and adjusting during learning. How can students develop more flexibility by monitoring and responding in the moment? Why is this responsiveness, instead of reactiveness, so important?

Adult tSEL

What is your relationship with flexibility? How can practicing flexible thinking support your well-being? Model the importance of flexibility by sharing your flexibility plan for the responsive cooperative learning lesson.

Motivational Moments

Responsive cooperative learning lessons offer a space to encourage students' motivation to learn and engage with content. Invite students to reflect on what boosts and motivates them during group activities. This boost of motivation supports self-management and increases well-being and joy in the classroom.

Activation: Using one of the Activation Tools on page 12, invite students to brainstorm what helps them feel motivated and excited to learn during responsive cooperative learning lessons. After discussing the academic goals and objectives of the day's responsive cooperative learning lesson, invite students to share aloud what about the lesson motivates them.

Reflection: At the end of the lesson, use one of the Reflection Tools on page 13 to provide time for students to talk about their experiences with motivation. How did motivation support their academic learning? How did motivation impact their focus? How did it affect the dynamic within their groups?

Make It Real

Grades PK–1	Grades 2–5	Grades 6–12
During the activation brainstorm, create a list of things that get students excited to learn. For example, "I get excited to try something new," "It's exciting and fun to work as a team," or "I get excited when we have new materials."	Invite students to consider what inspires them about learning. When do students feel inspired as learners? How do new materials impact their motivation? How does mindset impact their motivation?	Invite students to consider what sparks their interest in learning. When do students feel connected to learning and why? How can they work to find and maintain their excitement and motivation for learning?

Adult tSEL

What is your relationship with motivation? How can the practice support your well-being? Model the importance of motivation by sharing what motivates or excites you about the responsive cooperative learning lesson.

Strengthening Social Awareness to Cultivate Belonging

When we center belonging in social awareness, we can explore authenticity and ways to uplift it in our communities, large and small. Honoring authenticity—and being accepted as our authentic selves—has a deep and positive impact on our well-being and motivation in life. When you choose a strategy from this section and pair its tSEL lens with academic goals and objectives, you encourage this authenticity in your students (and yourself) during responsive cooperative learning lessons and beyond.

The Strategies

Other Views

Perspective-taking during responsive cooperative learning lessons encourages empathy and connection. Making intentional space to reflect on the views, feelings, and experiences of other group members fosters belonging and care. This cultivates social awareness.

Activation: Using one of the Activation Tools on page 12, invite students to brainstorm why it's important to consider everyone's thoughts, perspectives, and experiences during learning. After discussing the academic goals and objectives of the day's responsive cooperative learning lesson, invite students to share aloud how they can honor different perspectives during the lesson.

Reflection: At the end of the lesson, use one of the Reflection Tools on page 13 to provide time for students to share their experiences with supporting different views. How did perspective-taking impact their academic learning? How did it feel to put themselves in others' places? How did this strengthen connections within their groups?

Make It Real

Grades PK–1	Grades 2–5	Grades 6–12
During the activation brainstorm, offer the sentence stems "I think my group might feel . . ." and "I will support them by . . ." to help students brainstorm a list of other perspectives and possible responses.	Invite students to consider other times when they have included everyone's perspectives in a conversation. What did students learn about others? How did seeing a different perspective impact students' personal views?	Invite students to consider the complex emotions associated with different perspectives. How can students honor their groups' collective complex emotions during responsive cooperative learning lessons? How can different perspectives offer new learning pathways?

Adult tSEL

What is your relationship with perspective-taking? How can perspective-taking support your well-being? Model the importance of perspective-taking by sharing how you will be open and curious about students' views during the responsive cooperative learning lesson.

Strength Seeker

Responsive cooperative learning lessons are great opportunities for students to celebrate and uplift their peers, which helps them feel welcome and connected to the classroom. Discuss how seeing the good in others supports connection and belonging and develops social awareness.

Activation: Using one of the Activation Tools on page 12, invite students to brainstorm the collective strengths of each of their small groups. After discussing the academic goals and objectives of the day's responsive cooperative learning lesson, invite students to share aloud their groups' shared strengths in relation to the lesson.

Reflection: At the end of the lesson, use one of the Reflection Tools on page 13 to provide time for students to debrief their experiences with group strengths. How did it feel to have strengths named aloud? How did naming their group strengths impact their academic learning? How did group members' various strengths support the work they did together?

Make It Real

Grades PK–1	Grades 2–5	Grades 6–12
During the activation brainstorm, invite students to pause and think about the members of their small groups and to name some of their strengths. Offer the sentence stem "A group strength is . . ." For example, "A group strength is that we are kind to each other."	First pair students—whether within or outside of their small groups—and invite them to share strengths about their groups with each other. Then, come together as a whole group and invite sharing from the pairs.	First have students gather in their small groups and name three to five group strengths. Then, gather as a whole group to list collective strengths.

Adult tSEL

What is your relationship with identifying strengths in others? How can the practice support your own well-being and that of your group or community? Model the importance of identifying others' strengths by sharing students' strengths associated with the responsive cooperative learning lesson.

Employ Empathy

Responsive cooperative learning lessons provide a rich opportunity for students to develop and practice empathy, thereby strengthening their social awareness skills. The ability to understand the experiences of peers fosters connection and kindness. Invite students to listen to and honor the experiences of other members of their small groups.

Activation: Using one of the Activation Tools on page 12, invite students to brainstorm ways to be empathetic. After discussing the academic goals and objectives of the day's responsive cooperative learning lesson, invite students to share aloud the ways they can be empathetic during the lesson.

Reflection: At the end of the lesson, use one of the Reflection Tools on page 13 to provide time for students to share their experiences. How did hearing and honoring their group members' experiences impact their academic learning and their collective work? How did it feel to try to put themselves in others' places? How did it feel to have empathy extended to them?

Make It Real

Grades PK–1	Grades 2–5	Grades 6–12
During the activation brainstorm, offer the sentence stem "I am empathetic when I . . ." For example, "I am empathetic when I listen" or "I am empathetic when I think about a person's feelings." Consider using visuals (such as a picture of an ear or a heart) or additional explanation to scaffold students' understanding of empathy.	Invite students to consider stepping into another person's shoes. How can students honor another person's experiences? How does listening impact empathy?	Invite students to consider the complexities of honoring someone else's experiences. How can students affirm others' experiences and not interject their opinions? How can empathy guide their groups during cooperative learning lessons?

Adult tSEL

What is your relationship with empathy? How can empathy support your well-being? Model the importance of empathy by sharing how you will hear and honor students' experiences during the responsive cooperative learning lesson.

Center Compassion

Responsive cooperative learning lessons provide ample space for students to develop compassion and provide each other with support. When students act with care toward their peers, they develop community connections, amplify belonging, and build social awareness.

Activation: As a whole group, using one of the Activation Tools on page 12, invite students to brainstorm how to support one another and show compassion during group learning (and beyond). After discussing the academic goals and objectives of the day's responsive cooperative learning lesson, invite students to share aloud how they will be compassionate during the lesson.

Reflection: At the end of the lesson, use one of the Reflection Tools on page 13 to provide time for students to discuss their experiences with compassion. How did compassion impact their academic learning? How did it feel to give and receive compassion? How did compassion impact their small-group environments and interactions?

Make It Real

Grades PK–1	Grades 2–5	Grades 6–12
During the activation brainstorm, offer the sentence stems "If someone feels . . ." and "I will be compassionate by . . ." For example, "If someone feels confused, I will be compassionate by asking if they need help" or "If someone feels sad, I will be compassionate by asking how I can support them."	Invite students to consider the times when someone has shown them compassion. How did compassion make a difference in their lives? How can compassion make a difference in students' small groups during cooperative learning time?	Invite students to consider compassionate heroes in their communities. How can students show compassion in similar ways? How does compassion change the climate of their small groups?

Adult tSEL

What is your relationship with compassion? How can compassion support your well-being? Model the importance of compassion by sharing how you anticipate showing compassion to students and to yourself during the responsive cooperative learning lesson.

Gratitude Giver

Gratitude can help regulate our nervous systems, thereby supporting our collective well-being. Providing space for students to reflect on and name what they are grateful for during responsive cooperative learning lessons supports joy, connection, and social awareness.

Activation: Using one of the Activation Tools on page 12, invite students to brainstorm what they are grateful for in their classroom and school communities. After discussing the academic goals and objectives of the day's responsive cooperative learning lesson, invite students to share aloud what they are grateful for about the lesson.

Reflection: At the end of the lesson, use one of the Reflection Tools on page 13 to provide time for students to talk about their experiences with gratitude. How did it feel to talk about gratitude together? How did gratitude impact their academic learning and their group work? How might an increased awareness of what they're grateful for support them in the classroom and beyond?

Make It Real

Grades PK–1	Grades 2–5	Grades 6–12
During the activation brainstorm, offer the sentence stem "I am grateful for. . ." Invite students to reflect on the good things about responsive cooperative learning work. For example, "I am grateful for the chance to work with friends" or "I am grateful to have new classroom materials."	Invite students to consider the impact of gratitude on their bodies and mindsets. How do students' bodies feel as you list what students are grateful for? How do students' mindsets shift when they think about and name what they are grateful for?	Invite students to consider the role of humility with gratitude. How does naming what they are grateful for slow them down and help them be humble in the face of the abundance around them? How can gratitude change their lives?

Adult tSEL

What is your relationship with gratitude? How can gratitude support your well-being? Model the importance of gratitude by sharing what you are grateful for related to the responsive cooperative learning lesson.

Process Observer

Cooperative learning lessons provide an opportunity for students to work toward collective goals. When students act as process observers and provide feedback to each other about how their actions impact the group, they facilitate social awareness, belonging, and accountability.

Activation: As a whole group, using one of the Activation Tools on page 12, invite students to brainstorm a list of what a process observer could look for during a responsive cooperative learning lesson (for example, helping each other, everyone participating, using time wisely). After discussing the academic goals and objectives of the day's responsive cooperative learning lesson, invite students to share aloud the possible process observer feedback for the lesson.

Reflection: At the end of the lesson, use one of the Reflection Tools on page 13 to invite students to discuss their experiences with the process observer role—either as the person in that role or as a person receiving feedback. How did the process observer impact their academic learning? Was it difficult to provide feedback? Was it challenging to receive it?

Make It Real

Grades PK–1	Grades 2–5	Grades 6–12
During the activation brainstorm, offer sentence stems the process observer might use, such as "I saw . . ." and "Next time, we could . . ." For example, "I saw friends working hard to do their jobs. Next time we could be more caring when friends make mistakes."	Invite students to consider what feedback from the process observer will be most helpful to their small groups. What kind of feedback would help everyone feel like they belong? How can the process observer be kind with their growth feedback?	Invite students to consider the role of the process observer in developing a sense of belonging in groups. How might the process observer feel uncomfortable? How can the other group members support the process observer?

Adult tSEL

What is your experience with process observing? Have you practiced this skill with colleagues? How can process observing support your well-being? Model the importance of process observing by sharing how you will be checking in with groups as an additional process observer during the responsive cooperative learning lesson.

Honor and Accept Differences

Responsive cooperative learning lessons provide powerful opportunities to honor diversity in all forms and to accept every group member for exactly who they are. Each person, each brain, and each life is unique. When we honor this uniqueness, we strengthen social awareness skills and build a community of care, respect, and trust.

Activation: Using one of the Activation Tools on page 12, invite students to brainstorm why it's important to both honor and accept differences. After discussing the academic goals and objectives of the day's responsive cooperative learning lesson, invite students to share aloud the ways they can honor diversity during the lesson.

Reflection: At the end of the lesson, use one of the Reflection Tools on page 13 to provide time for students to share their experiences with intentionally honoring their differences and prioritizing acceptance. How did this impact their learning and group work? How did it feel to focus on extending acceptance to one another?

Make It Real

Grades PK–1	Grades 2–5	Grades 6–12
During the activation brainstorm, offer the sentence stems "Our differences make us . . ." and "In this classroom . . ." For example, "Our differences make us interesting" and "In this classroom, everyone belongs."	Invite students to consider their uniqueness. Why is it important to honor individuality? How can honoring our differences support our sense of belonging?	Invite students to consider the multiple ecosystems of our world. Every creature has a part to play. Why is it important to honor our classroom ecosystem? How can honoring our differences support our ecosystem?

Adult tSEL

What is your relationship with honoring differences? How can it support your well-being? Model the power of honoring differences by sharing how you embrace and accept differences (generally, not about specific students) during responsive cooperative learning lessons.

Opportunity Optics

Identifying fun learning opportunities fosters a realistic sense of optimism that supports risk-taking and perseverance. Talk with students about how pausing and thinking about the fun opportunities provided by a cooperative learning lesson supports their ability to get started, be confident, and feel connected with their group.

Activation: Using one of the Activation Tools on page 12, invite students to brainstorm the opportunities associated with responsive cooperative learning lessons. After discussing the academic goals and objectives of the day's responsive cooperative learning lesson, invite students to share aloud the possible opportunities during the lesson.

Reflection: At the end of the lesson, use one of the Reflection Tools on page 13 to provide time for students to reflect and share. How did anticipating fun opportunities impact the way they experienced the lesson? What effect did it have on their academic learning? Does that change the way they feel about their next cooperative learning lesson?

Make It Real

Grades PK–1	Grades 2–5	Grades 6–12
During the activation brainstorm, offer the sentence stem "We will have fun when we . . ." For example, "We will have fun when we make sure everyone has a turn."	Invite students to think about how learning opportunities impact their mindsets. When students consider opportunities associated with responsive cooperative learning lessons, how does that affect their mood and frame of mind?	Invite students to consider the importance of intentionally focusing on learning opportunities. How does that focus interrupt negativity bias? How does an "opportunity focus" inspire them?

Adult tSEL

What is your relationship with focusing on fun opportunities with colleagues? With your students? How can the practice support your well-being? Model the importance of this strategy by sharing the fun opportunities that you think will be part of the responsive cooperative learning lesson.

Community Celebrations

Responsive cooperative learning lessons support intentional space for students to celebrate each other. Talk with students about how intentionally celebrating each other increases their sense of belonging in the classroom and builds a community of care.

Activation: Using one of the Activation Tools on page 12, invite students to brainstorm how they can celebrate each other during responsive cooperative learning lessons. After discussing the academic goals and objectives of the day's responsive cooperative learning lesson, invite students to share aloud how they will celebrate their group members during the lesson.

Reflection: At the end of the lesson, use one of the Reflection Tools on page 13 to provide time for students to debrief their experiences with celebrating other students. How did celebrating their group members impact their academic learning? How did it feel to give and receive shout-outs? How can they regularly celebrate each other in ways that are both intentional and genuine?

Make It Real

Grades PK–1	Grades 2–5	Grades 6–12
During the activation brainstorm, offer the sentence stem "I can celebrate my group members when . . ." For example, "I can celebrate my group members when they take turns" or "I can celebrate my group members when they share their ideas."	Invite students to consider the little things. Remind them that even the simplest celebrations can be meaningful. For example, "Shout-out for always saying hi when the lesson begins. That makes me feel welcome in our group."	Invite students to focus on genuine compliments. How can they be authentic in their celebrations? How can students support each other if they feel vulnerable about sharing a celebration?

Adult tSEL

What is your relationship with celebrating others? How does it support your well-being? Model the importance of this practice by sharing collective celebrations about your students at the end of the responsive cooperative learning lesson.

Systems Support

The routines and systems you develop and agree upon with students during responsive cooperative learning lessons create networks of support that they can rely on. This supports the brain's predictive nature and creates a sense of safety. It also enables deeper engagement with content and fosters a feeling of trust and belonging, which in turn cultivates social awareness.

Activation: Using one of the Activation Tools on page 12, invite students to brainstorm the routines and systems that support them during responsive cooperative learning lessons. After discussing the academic goals and objectives of the day's responsive cooperative learning lesson, invite students to share aloud the systems that will support them during the lesson.

Reflection: At the end of the lesson, use one of the Reflection Tools on page 13 to provide time for students to reflect on their experiences with naming and accessing support systems and classroom routines. How did these systems impact their academic learning? How did their groups benefit from these supports?

Make It Real

Grades PK–1	Grades 2–5	Grades 6–12
During the activation brainstorm, offer the sentence stem "A support is . . ." For example, "A support is our materials cubby."	Invite students to consider the importance of reflecting on and refining support systems. What are the routines for responsive cooperative learning lessons? Are there systems that need to be adjusted? What systems help students feel that they belong?	Invite students to consider the impact of systems on their brains. When students can anticipate supportive systems, what impact does that have on their brains? Do students need to refine any systems to better center belonging?

Adult tSEL

What is your relationship with systems of support in your life? How can reflecting on these systems boost your well-being? Model the importance of reflecting on systems of support by sharing a routine or system you plan to access during the responsive cooperative learning lesson and how it will help you.

Strengthening Relationship Skills to Cultivate Problem-Solving

When we focus on relationship skills as part of collaborative problem-solving, we can explore how to honor the collective knowledge in our responsive cooperative learning groups and also in our wider communities. We strive to understand each other and to work together. When you choose a strategy from this section and pair its tSEL lens with academic goals and objectives, you encourage this collective understanding and teamwork in your students (and yourself) during responsive cooperative learning lessons and beyond.

The Strategies

Communicate Needs

Clearly communicating our needs and having those needs supported is essential to responsive cooperative learning lessons. Having intentional space to reflect and plan for clear communication supports collaborative problem-solving within the classroom and small groups. Anticipating our own needs and those of others, and planning to support those needs, builds healthy relationship skills.

Activation: As a whole group, using one of the Activation Tools on page 12, invite students to brainstorm ideas about what they may need during responsive cooperative learning lessons and how group members can support each other by meeting those needs. After discussing the academic goals and objectives of the day's responsive cooperative learning lesson, invite students to share aloud potential needs and supports for the lesson.

Reflection: At the end of the lesson, use one of the Reflection Tools on page 13 to provide time for students to share their experiences with communicating their needs and supports. How did sharing their needs and receiving support impact their academic learning? When students told their group members what they needed, what happened? How did this experience feel?

Make It Real

Grades PK–1	Grades 2–5	Grades 6–12
During the activation brainstorm, offer the sentence stems "I need . . ." and "I can help by . . ." For example, "I need more materials" and "I can help by sharing materials." Or, "I need extra time" and "I can help by waiting patiently."	Invite students to consider the importance of naming needs and supports. What would happen if students didn't name their needs? What would happen if students didn't support each other?	Invite students to consider the power dynamics related to needs and supports. Are all voices supported? What is the role of patience and understanding?

Adult tSEL

What is your relationship with communicating your needs? How can this practice support your well-being? Model clear communication by sharing needs you anticipate having during the lesson, as well as support you may offer.

Listening Power

Pausing to hear others' thoughts improves our ability to collaboratively problem-solve during responsive cooperative learning lessons. Tell students that when we truly listen to group members, we pause, consider their ideas, and respond from a place that honors them. We focus on the person who is sharing, not just on our own ideas that we would like to interject. This improves our relationship skills.

Activation: Using one of the Activation Tools on page 12, invite students to brainstorm powerful active listening phrases to use in their groups. After discussing the academic goals and objectives of the day's responsive cooperative learning lesson, invite students to share aloud the ways they can show they are listening to their group members during the lesson.

Reflection: At the end of the lesson, use one of the Reflection Tools on page 13 to provide time for students to debrief their experiences with listening. How did listening closely to their group members impact their academic learning? How did it feel to be heard by one another?

Make It Real

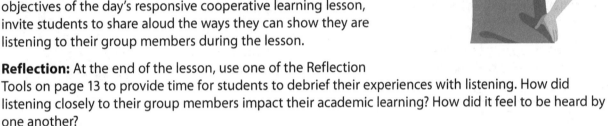

Grades PK–1	Grades 2–5	Grades 6–12
During the activation brainstorm, offer the sentence stems "I heard you say . . ." and "I have a question about . . ."	Invite students to consider the language they can use to communicate that they are listening to their group members. How will students acknowledge their group members' words? How will students ask for more explanation of group members' ideas?	Invite students to focus on listening phrases related to problem-solving. For example, "Your idea will help us by . . ." and "Please clarify what you meant by . . ."

Adult tSEL

What is your relationship with listening? How can listening support your well-being and your relationships? Model the importance of listening by sharing a listening statement you will use during the responsive cooperative learning lesson.

Body Language

Responsive cooperative learning lessons offer a space for students to collaboratively problem-solve ways of being together in a group. Talk with students about the idea of body language and what it can communicate to our fellow group members. Be sure to acknowledge that our body language is individual and based on our cultures. Remind students to honor one another to deepen their relationship skills.

Activation: Using one of the Activation Tools on page 12, invite students to brainstorm body language people might display during responsive cooperative learning lessons and what that might mean. After discussing the academic goals and objectives of the day's responsive cooperative learning lesson, invite students to share aloud the possible body language that might happen during the lesson.

Reflection: At the end of the lesson, use one of the Reflection Tools on page 13 to provide time for students to reflect on their experiences with body language. How did paying attention to body language impact their academic learning and group work? What did they learn about body language?

Make It Real

Grades PK–1

During the activation brainstorm, offer the sentence stem "When I feel . . . I might . . ." For example, "When I feel happy, I might smile" or "When I feel ready to keep working, I might give a thumbs-up." Remind students to honor that body language is different for everyone.

Grades 2–5

Invite students to reflect on their understanding of diverse body language and provide specific, individual examples. For example, some students might nod to show understanding, lean in when listening to someone, or stretch when feeling tired or in need of a break.

Grades 6–12

Invite students to discuss the ways body language varies and has different meanings for individuals. Encourage them to consider how to clarify and communicate about their own personal body language.

Adult tSEL

What is your relationship with body language? How can better understanding body language support your well-being? Model the importance of body language by sharing how you will use or pay attention to your own body language during the responsive cooperative learning lesson.

Conflict Kindness

Conflict is a part of life and a part of all relationships. Responsive cooperative learning lessons provide a safe and encouraging space for students to thoughtfully navigate the ruptures that occur in groups. Talk with students about the benefits of pausing and responding calmly and with kindness in mind.

Activation: As a whole group, using one of the Activation Tools on page 12, invite students to brainstorm ways to respond to conflict with kindness. After discussing the academic goals and objectives of the day's responsive cooperative learning lesson, invite students to share aloud the ways they can use conflict kindness during the lesson.

Reflection: At the end of the lesson, use one of the Reflection Tools on page 13 to provide time for students to debrief their experiences with conflict kindness. How did conflict kindness impact their academic learning? How did it feel to intentionally respond to conflict with kindness? How did it support the relationships within the group?

Make It Real

Grades PK–1	Grades 2–5	Grades 6–12
During the activation brainstorm, offer the sentence stem "When I disagree, I . . ." For example, "When I disagree, I use my words" or "When I disagree, I take three deep breaths to calm down."	Invite students to consider the importance of responding to conflict from a regulated place. How do students respond when they disagree with group members? For example, "When I disagree, I pause and think of what I am going to say before I start speaking."	Invite students to consider the importance of conflict. How can conflict help us learn and grow? How does engaging with conflict in centered ways support problem-solving?

Adult tSEL

What is your relationship with conflict? How can navigating conflict calmly and with clarity support your well-being? Model the importance of working through conflict by sharing how you regulate your own nervous system when engaging in conflicts.

Mentor Moments

Encouraging students to see themselves as mentors cultivates their confidence and relationship skills. Tell students that responsive cooperative learning lessons provide an opportunity for everyone to draw on their strengths and to be mentors to other group members who might not have as much experience or confidence in certain subjects or skills.

Activation: Using one of the Activation Tools on page 12, invite students to brainstorm ways they can be mentors to one another. After discussing the academic goals and objectives of the day's responsive cooperative learning lesson, invite students to share aloud the ways they can be mentors during the lesson. Then have each group choose someone to be the mentor for today's lesson (offering your support as needed).

Reflection: At the end of the lesson, use one of the Reflection Tools on page 13 to provide time for students to debrief their experiences with mentorship. How did mentorship impact their academic learning? How did it support their group work? How did it affect their problem-solving abilities?

Make It Real

Grades PK–1	Grades 2–5	Grades 6–12
During the activation brainstorm, offer the sentence stems "I am a mentor when . . ." and "A mentor . . ." For example, "I am a mentor when I help someone with a problem," or "I am a mentor when I share what I know."	Invite students to identify mentorship opportunities by considering group members' strengths. For example, they might know that someone is especially good at helping other people persevere during challenges.	Invite students to consider and discuss the differences between mentorship and management. How can mentors collaborate with their fellow group members as opposed to directing them? How does mentorship build and strengthen relationships?

Adult tSEL

What is your relationship with mentorship? How can being a mentor support your well-being? Model the importance of being a mentor by sharing how you will serve as an additional mentor during the responsive cooperative learning lesson.

Community Agreements

Community agreements support collaborative problem-solving during responsive cooperative learning by collectively naming ways of being accountable to each other. Discuss how it is important to create ways of being accountable that everyone feels comfortable with and everyone agrees to in order to ensure a community of care and to build relationship skills.

Activation: As a whole group, using one of the Activation Tools on page 12, invite students to brainstorm three to five collective classroom commitments. After discussing the academic goals and objectives of the day's responsive cooperative learning lesson, invite students to share aloud the specific community agreements that will be important for the lesson.

Reflection: At the end of the lesson, use one of the Reflection Tools on page 13 to provide time for students to debrief their experiences with community agreements. How did community agreements impact their academic learning? Their group dynamics? What might have been different if the community agreements didn't exist?

Make It Real

Grades PK–1	Grades 2–5	Grades 6–12
During the activation brainstorm, offer ideas, if needed. For example, "We will listen to each other" or "We will use kind words."	Invite students to consider community agreements that support problem-solving. What kind of language will they use with one another? What kind of actions will support fun for everyone?	Invite students to be both specific and ambitious in their agreements. For example, rather than "We will be respectful to each other," they might say, "We will honor and uplift everyone's individuality." Talk about what these commitments might look like in action.

Adult tSEL

What is your relationship with creating community agreements with your colleagues? How can the practice support your well-being? Model the importance of community agreements by sharing the community agreements you will focus on during the responsive cooperative learning lesson.

Kind and Caring Leadership

Leading a group with kindness and care supports collaborative problem-solving and deepens relationship skills during responsive cooperative learning. Talk with students about how leadership is important to their small groups, and share that each of them will have an opportunity to be a kind and caring leader.

Activation: Using one of the Activation Tools on page 12, invite students to brainstorm ways of exhibiting caring and kind leadership. After discussing the academic goals and objectives of the day's responsive cooperative learning lesson, invite students to share aloud how the role of a kind and caring leader might look during the lesson. Then choose a volunteer from each small group to be the leader of the day.

Reflection: At the end of the lesson, use one of the Reflection Tools on page 13 to provide time for students to discuss their experiences. How did having a kind and caring leader impact their academic learning? From the leaders' perspectives, how did it feel to lead with kindness? How did it help the group work through any problems they encountered?

Make It Real

Grades PK–1	Grades 2–5	Grades 6–12
During the activation brainstorm, offer the sentence stem "A kind and caring leader. . ." For example, "A kind and caring leader listens. A kind and caring leader helps the group share materials."	Invite students to consider how a kind and caring leader will affect their groups. How will the climate of their small groups be impacted?	Invite students to consider what they'd like a kind and caring leader to do, as well as how they'd like to act in this leadership role. How does thinking about the role from both sides help students develop their ideas?

Adult tSEL

What is your relationship with kind and caring leaders? How can this type of leadership support your well-being? Model the importance of kind leadership by sharing how you will be an additional kind and caring leader during the responsive cooperative learning lesson.

Helping Heroes

Responsive cooperative learning lessons center helping in service of learning. Discuss with students how their ability to help their group members strengthens their relationships, deepens their collaborative problem-solving skills, and supports their learning.

Activation: Using one of the Activation Tools on page 12, invite students to brainstorm ways to help and support their group members (and others!). After discussing the academic goals and objectives of the day's responsive cooperative learning lesson, invite students to share aloud the ways that they will be helping heroes during the lesson.

Reflection: At the end of the lesson, use one of the Reflection Tools on page 13 to provide time for students to talk about their experiences. How did being helping heroes impact their academic learning? How did it feel to help each other? How did it feel to be helped? How did it support their group's work and collaboration?

Make It Real

Grades PK–1	Grades 2–5	Grades 6–12
During the activation brainstorm, offer the sentence stem "I am a helping hero when I . . ." For example, "I am a helping hero when I clean up" or "I am a helping hero when I share materials with group members."	Invite students to think about people or characters who are heroes to them. How do they help others? How can students carry out similar helping actions?	Invite students to be creative in thinking about the many forms helping can take and to go beyond the tangible. For example, "I can be helpful by being joyful."

Adult tSEL

What is your relationship with helping? How can helping others support your well-being? Model the importance of helping by sharing how you will be a helping hero during the responsive cooperative learning lesson.

Seeking Support

Responsive cooperative learning lessons provide space for students to explicitly ask for support from each other. Asking for support and having needs met is critical to collaboration, problem-solving, and relationship-building. Acknowledge that asking for support can be difficult, so establishing trust among group members and knowing members will be there for each other is essential.

Activation: Using one of the Activation Tools on page 12, invite students to brainstorm ways they can ask each other for support when they need it. After discussing the academic goals and objectives of the day's responsive cooperative learning lesson, invite students to share aloud the supports they may need in relationship to the lesson.

Reflection: At the end of the lesson, use one of the Reflection Tools on page 13 to provide time for students to share their experiences with seeking support. How did asking for support impact their academic learning? How did it feel to do this? Did they learn anything they can use next time they need to ask for support?

Make It Real

Grades PK–1	Grades 2–5	Grades 6–12
During the activation brainstorm, offer the sentence stem "When I have a problem, I can . . ." For example, "When I have a problem, I can ask a friend to listen" or "When I have a problem, I can ask a group member to explain something again."	Invite students to gather in their small groups to brainstorm previous times they wish they'd had more support. For example, if they've struggled to process directions in the past, they could say, "I can ask a group member to talk through the directions with me one-on-one."	Invite students to gather in their small groups to discuss the vulnerability of asking for support and ways to move through that discomfort. It may be reassuring to remember that everyone needs support sometimes.

Adult tSEL

What is your relationship with asking for support? How can asking for support impact your well-being and strengthen your relationships? Model the importance of seeking support by sharing how you will ask for support during the responsive cooperative learning lesson.

Repairing Harm

Navigating conflict during responsive cooperative learning includes navigating repair. Discuss with students how repairing any harm they cause supports a community of care and deepens their relationship skills. We know conflict is a part of life, and knowing ways to repair harm we cause our group members helps us strengthen our connections to each other and create a path forward together.

Activation: As a whole group, using one of the Activation Tools on page 12, invite students to brainstorm specific ways they can repair harm when conflicts occur. After discussing the academic goals and objectives of the day's responsive cooperative learning lesson, invite students to share aloud how they can repair any harm that occurs during the lesson.

Reflection: At the end of the lesson, use one of the Reflection Tools on page 13 to provide time for students to discuss their experiences with repairing harm. How did repairing harm impact their academic learning? How did it feel to be intentional about repairing harm? How did it affect relationships and trust within the group?

Make It Real

Grades PK–1	Grades 2–5	Grades 6–12
During the activation brainstorm, offer the sentence stem "When I harm someone, I can . . ." For example, "When I harm someone, I can ask the person what they need" or "When I harm someone, I can promise to change my actions in the future."	Encourage students to be as specific as they can. For example, "I will take a break before taking steps to repair harm" or "I will ask the person how I can help make things right."	Invite students to discuss the idea of offering a genuine apology. As needed, support them in the discussion of what makes an apology sincere. For example, not making excuses; taking ownership of the harm caused; and committing to not repeat the harmful action.

Adult tSEL

What is your relationship with repairing harm? How can the practice support your well-being and that of your community? Model the importance of repairing harm by sharing how you will personally repair harm with students and how you will be available to help repair harm during the responsive cooperative learning lesson.

Strengthening Responsible Decision-Making to Cultivate Curiosity

An important part of responsible decision-making involves centering curiosity. When we do so, we can seek knowledge through openness and humility. This prepares us to explore and embrace different perspectives and impacts our engagement and motivation. When you choose a strategy from this section and pair its tSEL lens with academic goals and objectives, you encourage openness in your students (and yourself) during responsive cooperative learning lessons and beyond.

The Strategies

Curiosity Connections

Approaching decision-making from a place of curiosity encourages exploration and supports possibility during responsive cooperative learning lessons. Having intentional space and time to generate possible ways to complete a lesson can be joyful and fun.

Activation: As a whole group, using one of the Activation Tools on page 12, invite students to brainstorm possible questions they may consider when making group decisions about the responsive cooperative learning lesson. After discussing the academic goals and objectives of the day's responsive cooperative learning lesson, invite students to share aloud potential questions that spark curiosity for them and that they could use for decision-making during the lesson.

Reflection: At the end of the lesson, use one of the Reflection Tools on page 13 to provide time for students to share their experiences. How did the questions impact their academic learning? How did asking questions help their group make decisions before and during learning? How did it feel to approach decision-making with curiosity?

Make It Real

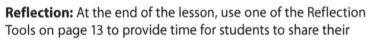

Grades PK–1	Grades 2–5	Grades 6–12
During the activation brainstorm, model questions for students if needed, such as "How can we listen to everyone's ideas?" or "What supplies will we need to collect?"	Invite students to brainstorm with their small groups first. As they do, encourage them to consider group dynamics. For example, "How will we make sure everyone is heard as we reach a decision?"	Invite students to engage with the complexities of learning through the lens of curiosity. For example, "How can we look at things in a new way when we are having trouble reaching a decision as a group?"

Adult tSEL

What is your relationship with developing questions associated with a learning activity? How does approaching tasks and decisions with curiosity impact your well-being? Model this practice by sharing a question that you will think about and act on during the responsive cooperative learning lesson.

Opening Your Mind

Responsive cooperative learning lessons invite students to open their minds to multiple ways of approaching tasks and making decisions. Explicitly tell students that being open-minded supports them in exploring possibilities and finding solutions. When we choose to be open-minded, we provide space for exploration and discovery.

Activation: Using one of the Activation Tools on page 12, invite students to brainstorm ways they can intentionally be open-minded during responsive cooperative learning. After discussing the academic goals and objectives of the day's responsive cooperative learning lesson, invite students to share aloud the ways they can be open-minded during the lesson.

Reflection: At the end of the lesson, use one of the Reflection Tools on page 13 to provide time for students to discuss their experiences with being open-minded. How did being open-minded impact their learning? Their group dynamics? How did it feel to intentionally approach decision-making with open-mindedness?

Make It Real

Grades PK–1	Grades 2–5	Grades 6–12
During the activation brainstorm, offer the sentence stem "I am open-minded when I . . ." For example, "I am open-minded when I get excited to learn something new" or "I am open-minded when I feel curious."	Invite students to brainstorm with their small groups first. Then bring groups together to share. How did groups' ideas differ? What do students think that says about the idea of open-mindedness?	Invite students to brainstorm with their small groups first. Encourage them to keep the idea of decision-making in mind as they generate their statements. For example, "I will be open-minded by considering other ways of solving problems."

Adult tSEL

What is your relationship with open-mindedness? How does the practice impact your well-being? Model the importance of being open-minded by sharing how you will be open-minded during the responsive cooperative learning lesson.

Observe and Respond

Responsive cooperative learning provides an intentional space for students to pause, observe, and respond when making decisions. Tell students that it is important to practice pausing, observing, and responding to their group members—as well as to the content of the lesson—from a place of slowed-down curiosity.

Activation: Using one of the Activation Tools on page 12, invite students to brainstorm ways they can observe and respond with curiosity. After discussing the academic goals and objectives of the day's responsive cooperative learning lesson, invite students to share aloud how they will be curious observers and responders during the lesson.

Reflection: At the end of the lesson, use one of the Reflection Tools on page 13 to provide time for students to share their experiences with being a curious observer and responder. How did being a curious observer and responder impact their academic learning? How did it feel to intentionally pause before observing and responding with curiosity?

Make It Real

Grades PK–1	Grades 2–5	Grades 6–12
During the activation brainstorm, offer the sentence stems "I am curious when I observe . . ." and "I am curious when I respond . . ." For example, "I am curious when I observe with my senses" and "I am curious when I respond with thoughtful words."	Invite groups to brainstorm their ideas for observing and responding with curiosity. If they have trouble getting started, offer examples, such as "I will pay attention with an open mind" or "I will respond by asking my group members questions."	Invite students to consider the differences between observing and watching, and between responding and reacting. How does curiosity connect to the skills of observing and responding?

Adult tSEL

What is your relationship with being a curious observer and responder? How does intentionally observing and responding from a place of curiosity impact your well-being? Model the importance of this practice by sharing a way you will observe and respond with curiosity during the responsive cooperative learning lesson.

Action Reflection

Cooperative learning provides opportunities for students to thoughtfully reflect on their actions and decisions during the lesson. Explain to students that reflecting on their actions helps them develop a flexible mindset and curiosity about how they might do things in new or different ways. Action reflection is the key to growth.

Activation: Using one of the Activation Tools on page 12, invite students to brainstorm reflective questions they can ask themselves during a responsive cooperative learning lesson. After discussing the academic goals and objectives of the day's responsive cooperative learning lesson, invite students to share aloud how they will reflect during the lesson.

Reflection: At the end of the lesson, use one of the Reflection Tools on page 13 to provide time for students to discuss their experiences with action reflection. How did action reflection impact their learning and their work as a group? Did this reflection give them new perspectives?

Make It Real

Grades PK–1	Grades 2–5	Grades 6–12
During the activation brainstorm, offer supports and examples, as needed. For instance, "Am I helping my group?" "Did I remember to ask if someone needed help before doing it for them?" "Am I listening?"	Invite students to join their small groups to brainstorm first. Assure them that reflective questions don't always need to be weighty or serious to be helpful. For example, "How will I help my group today?" is a simple and positive question.	Invite students to discuss how reflecting honestly on our own actions can be challenging. Encourage them to craft their reflective questions with kindness toward themselves. Remind them that reflection helps them grow—and that we all have room to grow.

Adult tSEL

What is your relationship with reflecting on your actions? How does the practice impact your well-being? Model the importance of reflecting on actions by sharing a reflection on one of your own actions, either before or after the lesson.

Deep Diving

Responsive cooperative learning lessons are an opportunity to think deeply and critically about our own actions. Deep thinking also opens our mind to new possibilities and boosts curiosity. Discuss how a deep dive into our choices supports our growth as group members and improves the well-being of everyone in the classroom.

Activation: Using one of the Activation Tools on page 12, invite students to brainstorm potential reasons for carefully considering their decisions during responsive cooperative learning. After discussing the academic goals and objectives of the day's responsive cooperative learning lesson, invite students to share aloud how they will deep dive during the lesson.

Reflection: At the end of the lesson, use one of the Reflection Tools on page 13 to provide time for students to debrief their experiences with deep diving. How did deep diving impact their academic learning? What did they find challenging or rewarding about it?

Make It Real

Grades PK–1	Grades 2–5	Grades 6–12
During the activation brainstorm, offer the sentence stem "Deep diving can help me . . ." For example, "Deep diving can help me learn from my experiences." Consider using a toy or visual, such as a snorkel, mask, and brain, to scaffold understanding of "deep diving" as thinking really hard, as though we're diving deeply into our brains.	Invite students to gather in their small groups to brainstorm. If they get stuck, invite them to think back on choices they've made in the past and think about what went well and what could have gone better. If they could go back, what might they ask themselves before making that decision?	Encourage students to consider how deep diving can help them make better decisions in the future, not only during their group work but in all areas of life. Also emphasize that this skill takes time and practice.

Adult tSEL

What is your relationship with deep diving? How could the practice impact your well-being? Model the importance of deep diving by sharing a way you plan to reflect deeply about your actions during the lesson.

Well-Being for All

Decision-making during responsive cooperative learning lessons give us an opportunity to center well-being for all. Share with students that when we consider everyone's well-being, we support our brains, our bodies, and our sense of connection to our learning environment.

Activation: As a whole group, using one of the Activation Tools on page 12, invite students to brainstorm ways to support their own well-being and that of their group members as they collaborate and make decisions. After discussing the academic goals and objectives of the day's responsive cooperative learning lesson, invite students to share aloud ways to support well-being for everyone during the lesson.

Reflection: At the end of the lesson, use one of the Reflection Tools on page 13 to provide time for students to debrief their experiences with well-being. How did focusing on everyone's well-being impact their learning? How did it affect the mood and collaboration of the group?

Make It Real

Grades PK–1	Grades 2–5	Grades 6–12
During the activation brainstorm, break the idea of well-being into three parts: brains, bodies, and hearts. For example, "We support our brains by asking questions. We support our bodies by taking deep breaths. We support our hearts by being kind."	Invite students to brainstorm in their small groups first. Ask them to consider what group members need to feel comfortable, safe, and eager to learn and use this as a starting point for their lists. For example, "We will create space to honor everyone's ideas."	Invite students to discuss the idea that well-being does not look or feel the same for everyone, and that it's important to be curious about others' wishes and feelings. Encourage them to talk with their group members about what they each need and want out of group work and shared decision-making.

Adult tSEL

What is your relationship with well-being? What might improve it? Model the importance of considering well-being by sharing ways you will support yourself and students during the responsive cooperative learning lesson.

Making an Impact

Responsive cooperative learning lessons provide an opportunity for students to make an impact with their decisions. Tell students that focusing on the impacts of their decisions during group learning supports a sense of satisfaction. Intentionally making choices that have a positive impact on our learning gives us a sense of purpose and helps us be open to new challenges and exploration.

Activation: As a whole group, using one of the Activation Tools on page 12, invite students to brainstorm ways their decisions can positively affect their learning and group work. After discussing the academic goals and objectives of the day's responsive cooperative learning lesson, invite students to share aloud the possible decision impacts that could occur during the lesson.

Reflection: At the end of the lesson, use one of the Reflection Tools on page 13 to provide time for students to share their experiences with decision impact. How did their decisions impact their academic learning? Did their group feel more inspired and engaged when they focused on the potential impact of a decision?

Make It Real

Grades PK–1	Grades 2–5	Grades 6–12
During the activation brainstorm, offer the sentence stem "We can choose . . ." For example, "We can choose to share with one another."	Invite students to consider the impacts of their decisions in relationship to what they would like to achieve. For example, "When we choose to refocus after getting sidetracked, our group makes better use of our time."	Invite students to engage with the reality that there will be times when our choices don't have the impact we hope for. How can students still learn from those experiences and be inspired to use their new knowledge?

Adult tSEL

What is your relationship with reflecting on how decisions make an impact in your life? How could the practice impact your well-being? Model the importance of decision impact by sharing a choice you'll make to impact your own success during the lesson.

Decision Direction

Anticipating the possible directions of a decision opens our eyes to possibilities and inspires engagement during cooperative learning lessons. Talk with students about how pausing to reflect on potential outcomes of a decision sparks collective curiosity and can lead to new discoveries during responsive cooperative learning lessons.

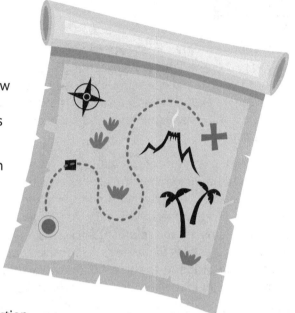

Activation: As a whole group, using one of the Activation Tools on page 12, invite students to brainstorm ideas about how decisions might play out during their group work. After discussing the academic goals and objectives of the day's responsive cooperative learning lesson, invite students to share aloud the possible places their decisions might lead them during the lesson.

Reflection: At the end of the lesson, use one of the Reflection Tools on page 13 to provide time for students to discuss their experiences with decision direction. How did the direction of their decisions impact their academic learning? Did they enjoy trying to predict what outcomes their decisions might have? Were they surprised by any of the actual results? How can they use this information going forward?

Make It Real

Grades PK–1	Grades 2–5	Grades 6–12
During the activation brainstorm, offer students an if/then framework. For example, "If we take turns, then everyone gets a chance to participate."	Invite students to be creative and think big! For example, "If we decide to make a video showing what we've learned, we might get to play it for the rest of the school."	Encourage students to discuss the idea that anticipating possible outcomes and consequences of a decision is not the same as being able to control what happens. Decision direction is about embracing possibilities, not seeking to limit them.

Adult tSEL

What is your relationship with decision direction? How could this practice impact your well-being? Model the importance of reflecting on decision direction by talking through possible outcomes of a decision you might make during the lesson.

Real Life

Connecting students' lived experiences to decision-making during responsive cooperative learning lessons makes the lessons relevant and engaging. Explicitly tell students that using their real-life experiences to make decisions during cooperative learning honors the experience and knowledge they bring to the classroom.

Activation: Using one of the Activation Tools on page 12, invite students to brainstorm helpful actions they do in their lives outside of school (helping others, listening when others have problems, including everyone in games, joining clubs that help their communities, and so on). After discussing the academic goals and objectives of the day's responsive cooperative learning lesson, invite students to share aloud the ways they can bring some of those real-life actions into the classroom to help their groups during the lesson.

Reflection: At the end of the lesson, use one of the Reflection Tools on page 13 to provide time for students to share what it was like to bring their real-life experiences into the classroom. How did it impact their academic learning? Did it strengthen connections within their group? How did it feel to share more about themselves?

Make It Real

Grades PK–1	Grades 2–5	Grades 6–12
During the activation brainstorm, offer students the sentence stem "In my life . . ." Encourage them to think of things they do outside of school that make them feel proud or joyful. For example, "In my life, I help others."	Invite students to brainstorm individually before joining their small groups to share. Do some of their real-life experiences overlap? Do they see a lot of variety in their experiences?	Invite students to talk about how sharing more about themselves with classmates can feel vulnerable. Discuss how being our whole selves can also be affirming and healing—but assure them that they don't need to share anything they don't want to.

Adult tSEL

What is your relationship with connecting out-of-school life decisions to your job? How could engaging in the practice impact your well-being? Model the importance of connecting real life to school by sharing how you will use your real-life experiences to support students during the lesson.

50 Strategies for Cooperative Learning—154085

Community Connections

When students connect their roles in community to decision-making during responsive cooperative learning lessons, they can experience joy and ease. Talk with students about how bringing their community roles into the classroom—and learning more about the community roles their group members play—supports well-being and connection.

Activation: Using one of the Activation Tools on page 12, invite students to brainstorm their community roles and how they can apply them to decision-making during group work. After discussing the academic goals and objectives of the day's responsive cooperative learning lesson, invite students to share aloud their community connections for the lesson.

Reflection: At the end of the lesson, use one of the Reflection Tools on page 13 to provide time for students to share their experiences with community connections. How did community connections impact their academic learning? How did the connections impact their group decision-making?

Make It Real

Grades PK–1	Grades 2–5	Grades 6–12
During the activation brainstorm, offer students the sentence stem "In my community, I . . ." For example, "In my community, I help others," "In my community, I clean up after myself," or "In my community, I say hi to my neighbors."	Invite students to discuss their community roles and how they'd like to apply those roles to their work together. For example, "In my community, I stand up for what I believe in. I'd like to speak up more often about things I really care about during cooperative learning."	Invite students to discuss the roles they play inside and outside of school. How and why do they differ? How might connecting their community selves and their school selves be beneficial? Does it feel challenging in any way?

Adult tSEL

What is your relationship with connecting your community to your job? How could doing so have a positive impact on your well-being? Model the importance of this practice by sharing the community connections you will use to support students during the responsive cooperative learning lesson.

Bibliography

Collaborative for Academic, Social, and Emotional Learning. n.d. "Transformative SEL." Accessed August 1, 2024. casel.org/fundamentals-of-sel/how-does-sel-support-educational-equity-and-excellence/transformative-sel.

Hammond, Zaretta. 2015. *Culturally Responsive Teaching and the Brain: Promoting Authentic Engagement and Rigor Among Culturally and Linguistically Diverse Students*. Thousand Oaks, CA: Corwin.

Johnson, David W., and Roger T. Johnson. n.d. "An Overview of Cooperative Learning." Accessed August 1, 2024. co-operation.org/what-is-cooperative-learning.

Learning Policy Institute and Turnaround for Children. 2021a. *Design Principles for Schools: Putting the Science of Learning and Development into Action*. September 2021. In partnership with the Forum for Youth Investment and in association with the SoLD Alliance. k12.designprinciples.org/sites/default/files/SoLD_Design_Principles_REPORT.pdf.

Learning Policy Institute and Turnaround for Children. 2021b. "Development of Skills, Habits, and Mindsets." September 2021. In partnership with the Forum for Youth Investment and in association with the SoLD Alliance. k12.designprinciples.org/development-skills-habits-and-mindsets.

Lin, Meiko, Svea Olsen, Dena N. Simmons, Miriam Miller, and Shauna L. Tominey. 2023. "'Not Try to Save Them or Ask Them to Breathe Through Their Oppression': Educator Perceptions and the Need for a Human-Centered, Liberatory Approach to Social and Emotional Learning." *Frontiers in Education* 7: 1044730. doi.org/10.3389/feduc.2022.1044730.

Minnesota Department of Education. n.d.-1. "SEL Implementation Guidance." Accessed August 1, 2024. education.mn.gov/MDE/dse/safe/social/imp.

Minnesota Department of Education. n.d.-2. "SEL Learning Modules." Accessed August 1, 2024. education.mn.gov/MDE/dse/safe/social/SELLearnMods.

Science of Learning and Development Alliance. May 2020. *How the Science of Learning and Development Can Transform Education*. soldalliance.org/wp-content/uploads/2021/12/SoLD-Science-Translation_May-2020_FNL.pdf.

Simmons, Dena. 2015. "How Students of Color Confront Imposter Syndrome" [Video]. TED Talks Live, November 2015. ted.com/talks/dena_simmons_how_students_of_color_confront_impostor_syndrome.

Srinivasan, Meena. 2018. "Social-Emotional Learning Starts with Adults." Association for Supervision and Curriculum Development, October 4, 2018. ascd.org/el/articles/social-emotional-learning-starts-with-adults.

Yoder, Nicholas, Angela M. Ward, and Sara Wolforth. 2021. *Teaching the Whole Child: Instructional Practices that Integrate Equity-Centered Social, Emotional, and Academic Learning*. Arlington, VA: American Institutes for Research. air.org/sites/default/files/2021-12/Social-Emotional-Learning-Equity-Centered-Instructional-Practices-December-2021.pdf.

Digital Resources

A list of digital articles associated with each strategy in the book is available on TCM Content Cloud.

Accessing the Digital Resources

The digital resources can be downloaded by following these steps:

1. Go to www.tcmpub.com/digital

2. Use the 13-digit ISBN number to redeem the digital resources.

3. Respond to the question using the book.

4. Follow the prompts on the Content Cloud website to sign in or create a new account.

5. The content redeemed will appear on your My Content screen. Click on the product to look through the digital resources. All file resources are available for download. Select files can be previewed, opened, and shared. Any web-based content, such as videos, links, or interactive text, can be viewed and used in the browser but is not available for download.

For questions and assistance with your ISBN redemption, please contact Teacher Created Materials.

email: customerservice@tcmpub.com

phone: 800-858-7339